INSIDE HUMOR

Exploring the Personal
Experience of Comedy
and Humor

GORDON ATLAS, PhD

Published by:
LAUGHING STOCK BOOKS
KEY WEST, FLORIDA

ISBN-13: 979-8-218-02278-5

Editing: Carol A. Rosenberg • www.carolkillmanrosenberg.com
Cover / interior: Gary A. Rosenberg • www.thebookcouple.com

Printed in the United States of America

To my parents, Ralph and Marlene. My father was the funniest person I've ever met, and my mother was the warmest and most supportive.

To my wife, Jana. She is truly a saint for coping with me for over forty years. I love you so much!

To my teacher, Dr. William Pizante. His wisdom inspired me to always pursue the truth, no matter how painful or difficult it may be, and challenged me to seek the highest level of understanding.

CONTENTS

WHAT IS HUMOR? BEGINNING THOUGHTS

The essence of humor has been of interest to researchers since at least the beginning of the twentieth century (Johnston, 1901); few works, however, are dedicated solely to its purpose. What is the basis of humor? What is the project of humor, as we might call it? What makes something funny? As we enter into the question of what humor is essentially, which is the primary focus of this book, another fundamental question must be kept side by side with the primary one as well, which is: Is humor a solitary thing? Is there an essence of humor that stretches across different domains? For example, is it the same to laugh at a person who slips on a banana peel as they walk into a room as it is to chuckle at the irony that one who pursued fortune and fame more vigorously and viciously than anyone is now bankrupt? Would this be the same as laughing when a child comes running into the room having forgotten to get dressed in front of company? Is there anything that ties together all these aspects of humor?

The two questions, moreover, are certainly tied together. If humor is one solitary thing, then we should be able to articulate how the various types of humor are related. In fact, it should then be possible to characterize types of humor on a continuum. Each would have a degree of whatever that essence of humor is or be a manifestation of the essence in a different way. Within the context of humor, though, there lies the most frightening and also the most exciting premise, and it is one that we cannot resist undertaking an exploration of: That humor can be classified in a *hierarchical* fashion, from most primitive to most advanced. Once articulated, however, the immediate dangers of such an undertaking become obvious.

The attempt to develop a hierarchy of types of humor is not only an ambitious enterprise but also one that is not the least bit politically correct in our present time. There is a common premise of equality, a laissez-faire regarding metaphysics, a tendency toward relativism when it comes to judgments about the arts. Pragmatism (Rorty, 1982) has pervaded even metaphysical discussions such that propositions are evaluated in terms of their *functionality* rather than their truth, and the assumption of equality pervades such notions. For one to even begin discussing a hierarchy of humor types is to entertain the notion that some humor is "base" and others more "noble"—which will invariably raise the eyebrows of those who wish to say that whatever one happens to find funny is simply their "preference" or, in essence, that humor is equally weighted.

Of course, the notion that humor lies on a continuum is, on the other hand, quite prominent in our everyday language about comedy and humor. "That's really primitive." "He has a really sick sense of humor." "That's so subtle that I'm not sure most people would get it." These are common utterances that imply our acceptance that some humor is, indeed, very primitive (dirty, dark, physical, simple, base) and that some is more sophisticated (subtle, clever, ironic, and deep). The language of "highbrow" or "lowbrow" humor is also demonstrative of this commonly accepted distinction between lower and higher forms of humor. Yet this claim has never been established or even examined systematically in the humor literature.

Many scholars, however, have focused on *peripheral* aspects of comedy and humor. Some have examined the social significance of laughter (Carroll, 2000) and the social aspects of the appreciation of humor (Weisfeld, 2006). Others have focused on the health benefits of laughter (Martin, 2001). Researchers have also studied gender differences (Gallivan, 1999; Lampert & Ervin-Tripp, 1998; Mickes, et al., 2012), age differences (Schaier & Cicirelli, 1976; Shammi & Stuss, 2003), and cultural differences (Erdodi & Lajiness-O'Neill, 2012; Nevo, et al., 2001) in one's appreciation of jokes and comedy. The focus of these studies has been, primarily, the *function* of comedy and humor for individuals and for society at large.

These studies, however, have not attempted to penetrate the heart of what is comedic. They have put the cart before the horse. If we understood the *essence* of humor, we could understand better the function and utility of comedy and humor. This investigation will situate itself inside the question of "What is comedic?" in examining a wide variety of levels of humor. Slapstick, for example, is commonly considered to be one of the most primitive, simple, and childish forms of humor (Freud, 1960), whereas irony, for example, is often held up as the pinnacle of comedic sensibility (Kreuz, 2020). The current approach will inquire into *the meaning* of humor as it is experienced. In that sense, we can say that the current approach is phenomenological and hermeneutic, examining the experience and meaning of humor.

Recent attempts to classify types of humor, moreover, seem to be particularly sensitive to the dangers of such a hierarchy and carefully avoid hierarchical typologies despite implying them at some level. For example, although the "affiliative" humor of Martin's (2007) classification is said to be the most functional, adaptive, and the healthiest form of humor, the authors of such work are careful to point out that we should not consider a certain form of humor (for example, negative humor) to be more primitive, more base, or less developed than the other forms.

The present work explores the possibility of a hierarchy of humor, but only in the context of understanding what the various forms of humor are and what humor really is, in essence. Since the question of what the essence of humor is has not yet been answered, we have been unable to develop a hierarchy of humor types. If such a hierarchy is, indeed, possible, the present work will, undoubtedly, serve as only a preliminary matrix. At the outset, we will simply proceed from the "commonly accepted" most primitive to most advanced forms of humor. So we begin with physical humor and conclude with irony and wisdom humor.

The categories of humor presented here have what cognitive psychologists call "fuzzy boundaries." Many of the jokes and humorous examples offered here work on several levels and employ more than one of the categories. For example, irony inherently involves incongruity and surprise. Observational humor often employs contrast and sometimes even dips into the realm of wisdom humor. The categories, however, are intended to be descriptively and intuitively useful, often shining light on the other categories and, most important, on the nature of humor itself.

A few words about the methodology employed in this book are in order. My own field of psychology has become infatuated with only one method, that of the empirical, quantitative method—the so-called scientific method. In this book, the method is primarily introspective, phenomenological, and exploratory. Of course, hypothesis production or exploration is considered a perfectly valid way of beginning to explore a field in which so little empirical work has been completed. The method used here probably needs no justification, and, for those bent on knowledge acquisition coming only from empirical studies, there is no violation here as long as no overstatement is made about the status of introspective inquiry.

I have, however, always been convinced that a kind of logical-intuitive introspection counts as knowledge as well. The tradition I enter into here, though, has gained more footing in the philosophical world than in my own field of psychology. As a young college student reading Merleau-Ponty (1962), Husserl (1900), Sartre (1943), and Heidegger (1927), I was taken by the phenomenological method of "pure description." Most compelling were the moments when Sartre or Heidegger described everyday experience in a phenomenological manner (Sartre, 1943). Sartre describes, for example, the experience of smoking or of skiing—how the smoker is able to "burn up the world" or the skier transcends ordinary reality by the act of "sliding." If we extend this inquiry to humor, we can ask, "What is the person doing when 'humoring' or when one is in 'comedy'?"

This is the aspiration of this book: capturing the "moment of humor" in the moment itself and revealing some aspects of what that moment is. I must say, though, that this method is not compelling for everyone. At its best, it is inspiring and revealing; at its worst, it may appear rambling, wildly speculative, and perhaps, indulgent. We can only hope for more of the former than of the latter.

If successful, however, this enterprise would provide the beginning of a much deeper study of humor. It would allow us to categorize and understand humor within the context of the phenomenological reality of the experience of humor and within the structure of a hierarchical matrix. Such a structure would, moreover, allow the connection between personality and one's taste in humor to be finally studied in a more systematic way.

The perception that has been prominent in my courses on comedy, then—that the type of humor a person chooses to engage in fits their personality very consistently—could be enriched by a language and an understanding of how that, finally, makes sense. In my experience, humor is one of the most diagnostic elements of personality—but we have, thus far, been largely unable to bring that intuition into the realm of substantive knowledge. This book is a first attempt to provide a structure that would allow such studies to thrive.

Keep in mind that the present work will attempt to **explore the possibility** of a hierarchy of humor, but only in the context of understanding what the various forms of humor are and what humor really is, in essence. The central question will remain for us: What is humor?

PART I

PRIMARY FORMS
OF HUMOR

Chapter 1

PHYSICAL HUMOR

Physical humor is defined as humor in which the comedic aspect is embedded in physical action (Wyer & Collins, 1992). It is nonverbal and immediate, seeming to require virtually no mediation or interpretation. The receiver's response, moreover, is generally very immediate. Physical humor is not the kind of humor that requires greater thought, more perspective, or an incubation period. It either "hits you" or it doesn't. In fact, the physical nature of the actors' portrayal of the humorous scene is mimicked by the receiver's response, which tends to be quite physical as well. Riotous laughter is usually the positive response, indicating that the person is "getting the joke." There are, however, those who simply do not get turned on by physical humor and find it to be silly, foolish, or inane. Others, on the other hand, will seek out this type of humor and may even find it to be their primary source of comedy.

Tickling

Perhaps the most primitive form of humor is found in tickling. There are some researchers (Leavens & Bard, 2016; Provine, 2014) who have examined the phenomena of tickling with some depth. But tickling is completely immediate and, largely, an involuntary response that involves explosive laughter. Some researchers (Blakemore et al., 2000) have attempted to address the question of why we cannot tickle *ourselves* but require others to stimulate the response. It is interesting that, starting with the most primitive experiences of humor, laughter and humor are largely based on social interactions. One can "amuse oneself" on occasion and enjoy a good comedy by themselves, but this is the rare case, indeed.

As humor, tickling requires the receiver to turn over control, voluntarily or involuntarily, to the tickler. Ishijima and Negayama (2018) examined mother-infant relationships and tickling. Ticklishness in young infants (five months to seven months old) was associated with more social behaviors, in general; the more ticklish children were also more social. It would be interesting to see the long-term implications of being ticklish as an infant on social behaviors and personality. It would appear that those children who are able to allow themselves to be tickled—who enjoy that form of humor—are also more interactive in social situations. Being ticklish might be a sign of a willingness or ability to relinquish control and enjoy humor, in general.

Key Elements in Physical Humor

Three elements must be present for physical humor to work; first, it must be the case that *you are not the one experiencing the encounter.* The distance inherent in being the *perceiver* is essential. If you are the one who falls on the banana peel, for example, it is not humorous—but those around you might find it exhilarating. The other participant in the physical humor is seen as "in it" and the perceiver is allowed to be in the "for-itself" (Sartre, 1943), observing and experiencing in a vicarious way. Second, *there must not be any serious consequence* to the antics of the slapstick event. Nothing is really "at stake" in that whatever occurs can be "washed off" or recovered from quite easily, despite the immediate loud sound, mild pain, or discomfort.

As a child, I remember marveling at how the Wile E. Coyote—an animated series villain, could fall off a steep cliff, apparently hundreds of feet down, and then emerge unscathed, time after time.

In real life, of course, that is not possible—so the object of physical humor must not be seriously injured. Of course, one way to accomplish this is to simply present fiction (a movie or skit that obviously does not represent reality). Finally, there must be a *real connection* between the actor's experience and that of your own such that a sympathetic relationship exists. Comedy often appears to rely on precisely this type of contradiction; the other must clearly be "other" but also somehow "you" in order for the comedic presentation to firmly engage the perceiver.

Let us, then, examine these three elements—distance, lack of consequence, and engagement—in greater detail. Could physical humor be funny when it happens to oneself? Well, one might argue affirmatively here that one's own slips and falls and awkward moments are, indeed, quite humorous, even to themselves. But the key here is that it is not funny to oneself funny to oneself at the moment of the incident. In fact, people will even say things like, "This will be really funny later on, when I think of it." Or "If this happened to someone else, this would be hilarious, but it's not funny when it's me." Later, they may say, "Now, when I look back on it, the incident is really hilarious, but at the time, it was quite painful." In the moment of actually experiencing a slip or a fall, you are "in it" and not able to appreciate the humor that may be accessible later on or to another. In this sense, physical humor is usually enjoyed from a distance.

But we cannot be satisfied by simply identifying the necessary components of forms of humor but are compelled to move beyond this and ask the question of why distance is necessary. At first blush, it's an obvious question—or answer, in that one can easily say, "If it happens to you, it's not funny; it's painful. But if it happens to another or if there is a time gap after it happens to you, you can laugh at it." But, in fact, the transparency of this truth is particularly useful in our underlying pursuit of the question of what humor is. In other words, let us ask the question a bit differently: If distance is a necessary condition for humor, then what does that mean about humor? For the moment, let us say that humor requires the for-itself—the perception of—rather than the in-itself of being in the moment. Just as Sartre (1943) argued that consciousness is consciousness of something we can say that humor is *laughing at something*. One cannot be simultaneously "in experience" and also laughing at it.

What, then, can we say about the *consequences* issue? Why is it necessary for no, or at least weak, consequences to occur to the target of physical humor? If someone slips or falls—in an awkward manner that is inherently humorous due to the loss of control that is exhibited by the target—why is it not funny if that target is seriously injured or even dies? Again, our tendency is to state the obvious; tragedy or injury is simply not funny. In fact, we often qualify an injury or condition in terms of a scale of seriousness. It is a "serious" injury or "it's not serious." How do we, then, walk the tightrope such that the situation involves an injury or a fall or a consequence—but not a serious one, such that we can laugh at the situation?

That is, of course, a bit of the art of comedy—a secret that the best filmmakers or comedy writers have mastered. But keep in mind that even the best examples of comedy are rarely experienced in a consistent or universal manner by the perceiver. Many people would leave a Charlie Chaplin film or certainly a Three Stooges episode saying, "Well, I just didn't find it funny." In many cases, this is because they saw the injuries incurred or the consequences shown to be, indeed, serious. In fact, we will see that physical humor probably has the most variable of audiences; some live for this type of humor, and others experience virtually no positive reaction from it whatsoever. Some level of distance, once again, seems necessary, and if the consequences of what one is observing are severe, it is hard to remain distant enough to find the situation humorous.

What about the third element, however, of engagement? It seems to, on the surface, fly in the face of the kind of distance and separation that we've seen as critical elements of successful physical humor.

> The comedian Gallagher was known to place a watermelon on a table and proceed to slam it with a sledgehammer, scattering the juices and pieces of the watermelon into the audience, much to the delight of his fans. (Gallagher, 2014)

This single act of physical humor embodies all three elements we've identified—assuming you are not sitting in the front row of the theater when Gallagher smashes the watermelon. It is happening to another, the consequences are relatively minor, and it is highly engaging. The engagement aspect is present because this is happening to us, the audience, right now in the present moment. You could have been in that front row. But those in the front row, at the Gallagher shows, seemed to be enjoying it the most, laughing the hardest. They have the greatest engagement. After all, they chose to be in that position—and the only damage could be a mild stain on one's clothing.

The three elements identified, however, upon examination, serve as only a skeleton model for the experience of humor. They are not *what is funny*, per se—but only preconditions that allow the possibility of physical comedy resulting in something humorous. If we were to leave the discussion as it is, however, we would have failed to penetrate the most essential aspects of physical humor and only identified the preconditions of humor. This would be akin to saying that a baseball game is played on a field, with nine players per team, and in a nice stadium; it would not say anything about what the game of baseball actually is. You'd have to watch a baseball game to find that out, right?

Let us consider some examples as a way of pursuing our goal, then, of penetrating "what is humorous?" in physical humor. Let's ask, "What is *the moment* of humor here?" in recognizing the awkwardness of a fall or slip. There are at least two types of physical humor that need to be distinguished. In one, the protagonist is portrayed as a kind of innocent fool. The most prominent Charlie Chaplin character, the Little Tramp—a young, naive, and awkward but somewhat pitiful tramp—is perhaps the prototype (*City Lights*, Chaplin, 1931; *The Circus*, Chaplin, 1928; *The Gold Rush*, Chaplin, 1925, etc.). In a more "realistic" manner, Woody Allen (and, to some extent, the Marx Brothers, especially Chico Marx) used this same figure. Buster Keaton also portrays a similar character in his silent movies of the 1930s (*Free and Easy*, Keaton & Sedgwick, 1930; *Parlor, Bedroom, and Bath*, Keaton & Sedgwick, 1931; *Passionate Plumber*, Keaton & Sedgwick, 1932, etc.). Essential to physical humor of this sort is that the audience must be thoroughly convinced of the character's *innocence* from the beginning. Let's take a look at some of these most prototypical heroes of physical humor.

Slapstick

Slapstick originated from a club-like object, a wooden slat that was used in commedia dell'arte (Hainsworth & Robey, 2005), an improvised form of comedy that was popular in 16th to 18th century Italian theater. A loud, smacking noise would occur when an actor struck another actor with a stick, with little physical damage resulting. This combination of a loud sound with minimal physical consequences is, in fact, a common formula in comedy, as we shall see. Slapstick comedy would not succeed, for example, if there were *actual* pain or serious injuries resulting from the antics involved. We cannot laugh at real tragedy but only at the peculiar form of "smoke without fire" that comedy relies on.

Slapstick appears to have begun in 16th century French comedy (Searles, 1925), became popular in 19th and 20th century American vaudeville, and then figured prominently in the early silent movies of Charlie Chaplin, Laurel and Hardy, and the Marx Brothers. We also find slapstick in animation—cartoons such as Tom and Jerry and Looney Tunes. There is a great deal of slapstick in the Jerry Lewis movies of the 1950s and 1960s. Physical humor, however, is still ubiquitous and commonly found in comedic TV, movies, and stand-up comedy as well.

What is it that slapstick engenders in the receiver, such that it has such a long and storied history? How does something that is so base, physical, and primitive provide great entertainment for the audience member? Our task, again, is to enter into the phenomenology of humor—the moment of humor—in order to reveal its nature. Of course, slapstick being the most physical, simple, and direct form of humor would, perhaps, be the most opaque and impenetrable form to examine and understand.

"It's just funny."
"It cracks me up."
"It's silly and stupid, but I love it."

These are the kinds of remarks that slapstick lovers are prone to make. But what is the "it" that they are referring to? We might start with the deviation from the ordinary that slapstick/physical humor provides. In most of ordinary life, we do not bump into people, hit them, fall over, slip, etc. Ordinary life is without the wild deviations that physical humor provides. Physical humor is more exciting, more stimulating, and certainly provides a relief from the everyday ho-hum existence that most of us experience. But is that enough? Is that the real explanation we're looking for? I think not.

Deviation itself is never enough for comedy or, for that matter, any form of experience. A deviation could be seen as a frightening aberration, for example. If a person falls as they are heading to the subway car and are dangerously close to the drop-off (or, as the British call it "the gap"), this is generally not humorous at all but instead rather alarming. A simple deviation may even be inconsequential and one that we may ignore because it represents nothing of significance; if two people bump into each other but neither is harmed, this may represent a deviation but one that inspires neither humor nor alarm.

Charlie Chaplin: *The New Janitor*

In *The New Janitor* (Sennett & Chaplin, 1914), Charlie Chaplin plays a physical laborer who is wielding a broom that he is on the verge of losing control of. He is a menial worker in a business with administrators carrying out their executive plans. As he marches down the hall, he unintentionally swings the broom back and forth, hitting an executive in the head. This stuns the executive, of course, but even further—as he begins to recover, Chaplin delivers another unintentional blow in his own effort to control the broom. In the simplest terms, this scene could be regarded as unfortunate or even tragic in that it results in injury to an innocent party.

But the incident is funny. Why? It is precisely because of the relationship between the menial worker (Chaplin) and the executive. But let us begin again with the hero, the Chaplin character. The audience must, first, be convinced that Chaplin—as the menial laborer—is of a pristine consciousness. He has no ulterior motives. He is completely innocent, simply trying to make a living but rather awkward and maybe a bit pitiable. His movements, however, are somehow both awkward but also fluid. He swings back and forth easily but without control. If we find this funny, it is because of our identification with the innocence of the Chaplin character.

The scene is now set for the authority to enter. It is crucial that the authority is portrayed as evil or as an irrational or unjustified authority. He is guilty of the *pretense of superiority*. The bumbling-fool worker who lacks the executive's position and wealth is able to provide us with justice, knocking the executive to the ground with the most unintentional of actions. We laugh because of the positions of the two individuals. We would not laugh, for example, if Chaplin had inadvertently hit a small child with the broomstick. But the *pretentious* executive is a perfect target and an enjoyable one as well. You can see here how brilliant Chaplin is as a filmmaker in portraying these characters, often in a silent format. How do we know that the authority figure is irrational, undeserved, arbitrary, and therefore evil? His posture, gestures, and movement style must reveal it. He moves in a jerky fashion; he holds himself up as more than he is. His posture is too rigid and his movements are stilted. We instantly dislike him.

The unjustified authority is hit by the broom. How does he respond? He is shocked and annoyed but, even more so, insulted and appalled. He looks down upon the Chaplin character as he tries to compose himself and return to his assumed position of authority. But it is even clearer now that his position is imposed and assumed—not natural. In his response to the first blow, he reveals himself even more completely as a phony. We like him less.

The audience member, on the other hand, is in a kind of quandary. We are uncomfortable with the blow, the injury, the pain of the striking of the man. We see Chaplin continuing to wield the broom in an out-of-control-manner, and we cringe. What if he strikes the man again? We tell ourselves that we can accept the first blow as it obviously caused no serious damage and, as we inferred before, appears somehow justified. But we cannot justify further violence. But what pushes the scene even further is the continued blows. Again, the key factor here is the response of the authority. If he responded in an understanding manner and viewed the incident as an innocent mistake, we would no longer "allow" further violence. But since he condemns the Chaplin character as a worthless, annoying worker, we are open to yet another incident.

Of course, it is also an artistic and strategic issue for the film-maker as to how much violence can be presented in this comedic scene. How much the audience will "allow" is not infinite. But the second and third incidents are critical because that is when the audience breaks into riotous laughter. It is as if the positions of the two characters are saying, "Not only is this going to happen once, but it is a permanent situation." As long as one is innocent and the other an irrational, unjustified authority, the amount of pain inflicted upon the latter is almost interminable. But it is not, because laughter and humor are always limited—a theme we will come back to at another point.

At a certain point, the audience will leave this "special state" that has been created by the brilliance of comedy and no longer be susceptible to the particular viewpoint that has been instilled. Timing is important with comedy, as all good comedians know, and part of timing is knowing when hilarious relief may become audience fatigue with repetition. The effects of repetition in humor have been studied in regard to advertising (Zinkhan & Gelb, 1990). We may assume that the same would apply in regard to humorous movies.

How are the physical consequences portrayed as harmless? Much of this is accomplished with the music employed. Although these movies are referred to as "silent films," there is a soundtrack used on a consistent basis. During the various Little Tramp romps, there is a vaudeville-like track that portrays a silly, fun, playful atmosphere, despite the serious business office in which the New Janitor works.

Finally, we must ask about the engagement factor. This is provided by the cuteness of the Little Tramp as someone with whom we can all relate. He's childlike, innocent, and likeable, although we often wish he'd stay out of trouble. He walks bowlegged, with feet awkwardly angled, looking around in a perfectly innocent manner. Moreover, he's the only character the audience can really relate to because the other characters are all portrayed as "too serious"—stiff, pompous, and foolish. The main executive is later revealed to have some rather severe gambling debts that he cannot pay, which in one fell swoop demonstrates a major flaw, a vulnerability, and an impulsiveness that lies beneath his pompous and overly serious persona.

Buster Keaton: *The General*

Buster Keaton (Bruckman & Keaton, 1926) utilized train scenes as a very prominent device in his physical humor. As with Chaplin, these scenes were aided by the use of music—music that portrayed a playful, wild, romping nature that allowed the audience to enter into situations that would otherwise appear as very dangerous as comedic. The common theme in these train scenes is a series of continuing foiled efforts that lead to the very edge of possible catastrophe, followed by a narrow escape—and the cycle returns again.

Keaton's character begins by trying in vain to start the train. When he finally succeeds in getting the train rolling, his efforts lead to his being on the ground and not noticing that the train is moving. He then has to make a heroic effort to jump on the train, but, given the circumstance, he cannot be in anything but a compromised position on the train, as he barely makes it aboard. This, in turn, leads to a continued effort to board the train in a satisfying manner, leading to a series of near-catastrophic episodes. He sees a potential danger arising from a piece of wood on the tracks as the train is approaching, so he dashes off the train and tries to remove that obstacle but struggles to do so—until, just in the nick of time, he succeeds. At that very moment, however, a new, potentially dangerous situation arises, which the Keaton character must address.

Are we engaged? Yes—because the character is humble and innocent. He's not as pathetic and cute as Chaplin's the Little Tramp but has many of the same characteristics nevertheless. We sympathize with Keaton as one who simply needs to get this train moving and stay on it but runs into considerable difficulties in doing so. As each new danger approaches, we "buy in" to Keaton as a character and are rooting for him to escape, unharmed, but fear this may not happen.

There is, of course, another dimension of comedy that enters into the Keaton train romp that is so obvious that it may go unnoticed but plays a primary role in our experience: It's a playful adventure. The element of play cannot be overlooked. It is almost akin to tickling producing laughter. You sometimes see children giggling as they're playing. Play is fun, freeing, and funny. Why? Mainly because of the relief it provides from seriousness. The romp on the train is a funny adventure that we live, vicariously, through Keaton. If there is a message here, it is that we are too often cooped up inside, required to do things that are not chosen and take it all too seriously. Playing on the train is a freeing experience—especially when the consequences are not our own.

But why the train? Why are trains or machines so appealing for physical humor? Chaplin's scenes in *Modern Times* (Chaplin & Chaplin, 1936) present "the machine" as a foil for great comedic relief as well, as he is virtually consumed by the various machines he encounters at the job. The train provides Keaton with an even more promising vehicle, though, because it *moves*. But even more primary is the nature of a train as a huge machine that towers over the little person and overwhelms him. It is a version of a monster, yet freed from any human capacity, which brings the humanity of Keaton into relief by contrast. Being small is certainly an asset for Chaplin and Woody Allen, and though he is not as diminutive, Keaton presents himself as small in relation to the train.

What Keaton portrays in *The General* (Bruckman & Keaton, 1926) about the machine—perhaps foreshadowing Chaplin's semi-political attack in *Modern Times* (Chaplin & Chaplin, 1936)—is the dual nature of machinery for us. It is big, powerful, and certainly useful in propelling us to places with alacrity. But it is also dangerous, mechanistic, and on the verge of being out of control. It is this sense that we have of machines—that they are not fully within our control—that the comic plays with. Again, when we're "in" the experience of dealing with a machine that is not under control, it is frustrating and annoying or even maddening. When we can vicariously identify but also distance ourselves from the experience, it can be extremely humorous. The train is a particularly good choice because it appears to be unstoppable. Once rolling on the tracks, it is singly destined for continued motion—and our efforts to stop it are seemingly futile. Keaton, then, must negotiate within that realm. In more sophisticated, text-based comedic work, we might call this the preconditions or *premise* of the comedic story. But that is all portrayed *physically* by Keaton.

Also, the small versus large contrast utilized here is a very common ploy in humor. Think of the numerous examples of small children, often used in television commercials, who are talking in a way that defies their age and capability. They might be consulting on a financial investment, arguing for a certain product (which is not intended for children, like a car), or suggesting something that is not appropriate to their age group. The small confronting the large is, indeed, one of the most common forms of encounters that can be presented in comedy.

Abbott and Costello

In another example of slapstick comedy, *Buck Privates* (Gottlieb & Lubin, 1941), Lou Costello portrays a silly, overweight, and out-of-shape private in boot camp. At one point, he is thrust into a boxing ring and forced to fight a very powerful boxer. The expressions of fear and loathing that appear on Costello's face as he meets this formidable opponent are quite hilarious in and of themselves. Childishness in a man is the source of much humor. The contrast between the man's adult body and childish fear that is more befitting of a 5-year-old is another form of disarming humor. We are allowed to view him as funny precisely because he refuses to take himself seriously. He is, consistently, goofing around and being silly.

At first, Costello is taking quite a beating from the legitimate boxer. This is funny but not a peak "punchline"; rather it's a setup for the ultimate punchline (excuse the pun here). The peak comes as the lesser boxer finds creative ways to "allow" the better boxer to "beat himself." But the key factor is that, although Costello's opponent is legitimate in some sense, he is also stuffy, self-indulgent, and thoroughly unselfconscious. This makes it possible to laugh at this character and take joy in his demise, especially because it is self-inflicted.

The moral of the story—in the boxing match—seems to be that the fool is, in fact, more compelling and even more legitimate than is the "straight man" opponent. This is because the viewer grants him this status on the basis of his authenticity, over and above that of the opponent, who is viewed as insincere. A large part of the insincerity we perceive is based on our perception that he is taking life too seriously. Costello is the *everyman*, recognizing both the dangers and absurdity of boxing, whereas the opponent is, through and through, a boxer and therefore, in Sartre's (1943) terms, in bad faith. We, as viewers, join with the underdog because he is sincere and very human. His victory is relished since it demonstrates that humanity wins out over the in-itself trappings of unselfconsciousness. A hearty laugh is therefore "allowed."

One cannot help but notice, too, the element of irony inherent in the slapstick comedic event just described. The serious boxer loses precisely because he takes the event too seriously. He is overly ardent, too dead serious. It is, therefore, ironic that the one who desires victory the most and is the more competent boxer is thus defeated—precisely because of his overly serious attitude. The one who is cavalier, jocular, and silly, on the contrary, winds up, ironically, succeeding. The point here is that humor, even slapstick, is filled with narrative, purpose, and meaning.

Jerry Lewis: *The Nutty Professor*

We would be remiss in discussing physical humor without mention of one of the greatest physical comedians, Jerry Lewis. Lewis's persona is somewhat akin to that of the Little Tramp—a goofy, childish person who is obviously disarming. This is perhaps why parents could always count on a good, healthy comedic experience when taking their children to see a Jerry Lewis movie in the 1950s and 1960s. His greatest comedic achievement, though, may have been his directing and starring in *The Nutty Professor* (Glucksman et al., 1963), which was also remade, with Eddie Murphy as the star (*The Nutty Professor*, Lewis & Shadyac, 1996). The professor—the prototypical nerdy, goofy, childish Lewis character—is a scientist who happens upon a formula that transforms him into a sly, cool ladies' man who is charming and attractive but is completely lacking in moral character.

It is this contrast between the "nerd" and the "player" that forms the crux of the film and the story. Contrast, of course, is a central factor in humor. In fact, "incongruity theory" is one of the most prominent current psychological theories used to explain humor, as discussed by Zhan (2012) and will be examined in a later chapter. In this case, though, Lewis portrays this contrast in a largely *physical manner*. The movements, the gestures, the style in which Buddy Love carries himself reveal the smooth character that he is. The audience, however, is aware that Mr. Love is somehow still the nerdy, nutty professor, just in a different guise. How can opposites be one? Well, in human life, this is not surprising, and again, the comedic presents a human truth: There are distinct sides to a person that are often in stark contrast, like archetypal polarities, in a kind of yin-yang relationship.

What *The Nutty Professor* tells us is that there are two types of people, one that is unassuming, naive, childish, and goofy with obvious flaws but with a virtuous character. The "player," on the other hand, is devastatingly handsome, smooth, confident, and composed but has only their own needs in mind. We like both characters but wish that the best of each could be present without the negative side of each coming along with it. The humor is stricken by the sense of just how crazy it is that these two sides both exist within the same person! Also, there is a good deal of drama about aspects of the professor emerging during the smooth operation of the "player," thus ruining his "act." We're on edge about that—hoping that the professor's silliness does not spoil Buddy's wonderful, cool style but laughing when it does. That breakthrough of the professor's voice and style during Buddy's act is precisely what tells us that, indeed, this is one person while also providing the comedic action. We know the danger of this intrusion—that the player will not succeed with these intrusions. It is this anticipation that drives the comedy.

In the end, though, we are led to see that, despite his appeal, Buddy Love is an insubstantial and invalid figure, and the professor reemerges as the solitary, morally sound person, albeit with all his flaws and weaknesses. The moral seems to be one of authenticity and sincerity—again, a common theme for comedic films. You must be yourself, even if you are not as handsome and smooth and debonair as you'd like to be. All is returned to sanity, and the professor lives on in his flawed but sincere state.

The Three Stooges

The Three Stooges (McCollum & White, 1930–1970) was a comedic force in the 1950s that used a great deal of physical comedy as well. Moe, Larry, and Curly were hardheaded buffoons who were constantly getting themselves into trouble, arguing, and slapping each other around. There was, however, in contrast to the popular modern show, *Jackass,* (which we will discuss later) a storyline and some character development involved, minimal as it was. But again, we could view the popularity of *Jackass* and other such shows as akin to the popularity of the Three Stooges in its time. This is physical humor in its most primitive, male-oriented, aggressive form. Another difference, of course, is that the Three Stooges was staged and was theater, whereas *Jackass* is "reality TV."

But again, what is satisfying about seeing someone leveled by a prank set up by their friends? In some ways, it allows the viewer to experience some of their greatest fears vicariously and therefore without consequence. There are four levels of separation from the experience: It is "not you" since it's on-screen. It is not taking place "now" because it is filmed, and it is not "you" because you identify with the prankers and not the pranked. Finally, we can be reasonably sure that no great consequence will arise—the pranked will emerge basically unscathed. Generally, the victim is faced with a physical but also mental indignity where they encounter the impact of a physical force of some sort and are struck down but, again, never terribly injured. The relief for the viewer, then, is in seeing their own worst fears lived out with all those degrees of separation firmly in place.

There is, though, a kind of guilty pleasure in laughing at these escapades. One may even feel a touch of guilt because one knows that the laughter is coming at the expense of the victim who is experiencing the "torture" itself. Of course, those four levels of separation allow for the proper distance to emerge, which facilitates the comedic experience—for those who can indulge in this form of comedy. Many cannot. If there ever was a serious question about the strength of gender differences when it comes to aggression, the *Jackass* phenomenon should put that question to rest! In accordance with gender differences in relation to aggressive humor, Dyck and Holtzman (2013) conducted a study in which they found that aggressive humor styles generally had more support among men than women. Interestingly, Swani and his colleagues (2013) studied differences in regard to the appreciation of violent humor used in advertising. Women had more negative reactions to violent humorous advertising than men.

While the aggressive form of physical humor is perhaps epitomized by the Jackass series most recently, it has its roots in TV series such as the Three Stooges. Moe, Larry, and Curly were all buffoons, but Moe was the top dog of the operation, controlling the action and often playing pranks on the other two in which some physical pain would be the (somewhat deserved) outcome for the victim. Spaces between the physical aggressive interludes were filled by subplots in which the threesome found themselves in more or less serious trouble and managed to make things even worse by their idiocy, clumsiness, or inattentiveness. Then pain and suffering would ensue, with the victim either one of their adversaries or Moe or Larry themselves. There was a playful quality to their romps but no laughter from the characters themselves. The humor lay completely within the viewer (if the viewer was a fan of this sort of comedy).

What was the attraction? Well, again, this is a strongly male-dominated form of humor with a predominantly physical, aggressive character. The immediacy of the physical is one of the powerful draws, of course. The viewer would both identify with the Stooges and also maintain their distance as the Stooges entered into trouble after trouble. Viewers enjoyed the escapades vicariously and always feared the worst consequences would ensue—and they generally did. At that point, one could retreat into distance and laugh at just how stupid, foolish, and goony these guys were. A kind of justice, thus, is found in physical humor with the buffoon being the victim. In fact, trouble generally arose from the Stooges' interest in gaining some advantage over others without wanting to pay the price for it—stealing, tricking, etc.—so that when their own desires caught up with them and they were leveled for those desires, the viewer may feel that justice was served. Once again, there is more to physical humor than just the physical; psychological and moral dimensions enter into one's enjoyment of this form of aggressive humor.

Without empirical research to back up our claims, we can speculate that, again, the viewership for the Three Stooges was largely young males who were fulfilling a tendency toward an aggressive, physical form of humor. We now know that the catharsis theory of experiencing aggression is not supported, though; viewing aggressive content does not reduce the amount of aggression in the viewer. Does viewing such aggressive, physical humor lead to *more* aggression in the viewer? Quite possibly—but such a discussion would take us far from the central question of our task here. Suffice it to say that those who cite the Three Stooges and/or *Jackass* as their favorite forms of humor probably are revealing something of their physical, aggressive nature—even if it is not expressed directly in their personality.

But what about the other form of physical humor in which the protagonist is not the aggressor, per se, experiencing an aggressive victory, but the victor in the form of the clown, the fool, Chaplin's Little Tramp? On the surface, this form of humor invokes less aggression and more "humanity" in that we sympathize with the plight of the vulnerable protagonist and root for his success as he battles the powerful elements he encounters. In fact, a chief difference is noted here: There is a picture of society that is portrayed in the Chaplin mode of physical humor. Remember that in *The New Janitor*, the context is that of an overly serious business in which executives hold themselves in a stuffy, artificial manner—above the common person.

We are going to say that this form of physical humor, with the weak, vulnerable, childlike hero making a nuisance of himself, is not as purely aggressive as that of the *Jackass* and the Three Stooges variety of physical humor. In the Chaplin mode, aggressive acts are *unintentionally* committed against the invalid others—and we are allowed to laugh at the enemy (e.g., the puffed-up executives). The brilliance of Chaplin lies in his depiction of the unjust system and his inadvertent exposure of that system by its deconstruction in physical humor. What type of person would enjoy this type of humor? The audience for this type of humor is more sophisticated, of course—but that is only a cursory answer to the question. We might say that this form of humor has broader appeal in that all genders seem to equally enjoy this type of humor. But what are the personal elements that would predict the enjoyment of inadvertent physical humor? One obvious answer would be that it appeals to those who seek relief from oppression by society. The laughter is an escape from that oppression, a release from it as one finds a victory of the underdog in this form of physical humor.

Everyday Physical Humor

The video realm is not the only medium in which physical comedy occurs. In everyday life, there are constantly ripe appearances of physical humor. Let's examine the most classic occurrence of physical humor in some detail: A person enters the room, slips on a banana peel, and falls awkwardly to the floor. Is this funny? Of course, humor always depends on not only a target or stimulus but also a subject or receiver. For the receiver to find a slapstick action to be humorous, however, certain contextual aspects must be considered. For example, if the target person is an old, stuffy professor who insists on formality, his slipping and falling awkwardly could be hilariously funny. If, on the other hand, the "slipee" is a disabled person who already walks with a cane due to cerebral palsy, it would not be funny at all. The fact that the target of slapstick humor determines the comedic valence of the situation already illustrates the contextual nature of humor. McGhee and Duffey (1983) conducted an interesting study which showed that children between 3 and 6 years of age found humor that victimized a *parent* funnier than when the humor victimized a *child.*

Let us assume, though, that the target is the stuffy old professor who demands formality, good posture, and punctuality even when it is unwarranted. What is funny about the professor being leveled to the ground by an inadvertent slip? The essential meaning is right in the leveling, though, for the slip satisfies our need to bring him down to our level by forcing him to recognize his own "creature-ness." The slipping is also revelatory in that it reveals the way in which, despite his lofty attempts, he is not "above us" but simply another human being. This is captured by the slip. In the moment of slipping, he is caught in that contradiction. In everyday life, he turns his nose up at the common people but this attitude, insofar as it leads to not looking down at the floor as he enters the room, becomes his downfall. A kind of justice is therefore revealed in his fall.

The Meaning of Physical Humor

Physical humor, then, is actually filled with meaning—of culture, of politics, of social comparison, of human fate. In what sense, then, do we consider this a rather primitive form of humor? First, physical humor is nonverbal. It lies below the level of verbalization, at the level of action. But the perception of action is itself imbued with a great deal of meaning. That meaning may be *immediate* in the sense that is imbedded in physical action, but that, clearly, does not mean that it is lacking in cognitive content. We are reminded here of the Lazarus-Zajonc (Lazarus, 1981; Lazarus, 1982; Lazarus, 1984; & Zajonc, 1980; Zajonc, 1981; Zajonc, 1984). debates of the mid-1980s when the question of the primacy of affect (versus cognition) was raised in the psychological literature. The debate was never fully resolved, but the field has "moved forward" with a greater awareness of how *immediate* responses to stimuli can be.

Why, though, is most physical humor biased toward the underdog? Is humor reliant on a specific set of social-political beliefs? For example, would it be humorous if the *little tramp* was inadvertently hit in the head by the executive? A quick glance at other forms of humor—namely, aggressive humor—would tell us that much humor orients itself toward the denigration of what would be considered lower or baser, in favor of the dominant social group. Does physical humor, though, allow for this domination of the stronger over the weak? Perhaps—but the joy of slapstick and most other physical humor appears to be primarily based in the overcoming of the dominant by the weaker. It is a *mischievous* form of humor in its very essence. Physical humor seems to be the way in which the lower "levels" the higher, by a twist of fate in which the higher is forced to recognize its indistinction from the lower. In that sense, physical humor does seem to favor a particular social-political standpoint.

The Role of Physical Humor in Evolution

But let us now look at the other primary question that personologists pursue—that is, what role does physical humor have for an individual? As mentioned previously, there is a wide range of interest in this form of humor. Some will watch *Jackass: The Movie* (Tremaine, 2002), *Jackass Number Two* (Tremaine, 2006), and *Jackass 3D* (Tremaine, 2010) several times over and exclaim that these are the funniest films they've ever seen, whereas others will not be able to watch more than five minutes of this type of comedy and are even appalled and disconcerted by the fact that others do find this type of humor to be funny. Not surprisingly, the love of aggressive physical humor does seem to be correlated with an aggressive personality style (Markey, et al., 2014).

At this point, our distinction between aggressive physical comedy and self-deprecating physical comedy is, of course, necessary.

Since some would say that aggressive physical comedy is indeed the most primitive of all humor, let's examine that first. In fact, as John Morreall (1983) points out, some theorists have proposed that the very first humor probably occurred when one caveman, seeing another with something of interest (like an attractive woman), approached the other caveman, hit him over the head, stole the "possession," and enjoyed a hearty laugh. Although we cannot doubt the primitive quality of this form of humor and cannot attest to its temporal primacy in history, this is an intriguing theory of the origins of comedy. Moreover, it acts as a very good genotype for the beginnings of physical humor.

Despite its awful connotations for the human spirit, we must admit that the "thrill of victory," as unjust as it may seem in this example, is often accompanied by a hearty laugh. As you watch a football game and "your team" intercepts a pass, you might exclaim, "Ha ha! You see how that guy just came across and stole the ball from that other guy? Ha ha! Hilarious!" Of course, in this case, it is clearly not funny to the victim but only to the victor and those who identify with him.

What, then, is the victor (and those who identify with him) laughing at? At first blush, one might be tempted to say that this is, in fact, not even humor but a laugh that is based on hegemonic power. Its nature is so far removed from the laughter that occurs from hearing a witty story that we may wish to say that the laughter that emerges from the victory just described does not count for humor but for something else. What that something else might be is unclear, but maybe it's akin to a grunt or a groan or an exclamation. But upon further review, it is hard to deny that laughter is present here, and we are forced to consider its origins and place in the scheme of humor. In fact, this primitive exclamation of victory is humor—but of a physical, aggressive form. What is its meaning?

Again, central to this form of humor is the victim, who is seen as somehow "inside" of a delusion. He thinks he has possession of a woman but, in the violent act that becomes comedic, it is revealed that this possession is illusory. "Illusion revealed" is humorous in itself—so, for example, if the woman disappeared or turned out to be a figment of his imagination, this might be humorous. But let's not forget that this is not the essence of the primitive scene we are here describing. Notice that there is a dual emphasis on the victim's plight and the status of the aggressor; there is no question about the fact that we are *laughing at* the victim. But the victory is what is sweet. "I had no woman and was in distress about that, especially when I saw another who was in possession of an attractive one. Now I have one! And you don't! Ha ha!" The transcendence of one's state from lacking to fulfilled is precisely what one is celebrating with laughter here. The change of fortune—achieved with so little effort—is what is celebrated.

People Who Find Physical Humor Particularly Entertaining

What does the foregoing say about one who finds this form of humor attractive or entertaining? Simply that they are in desire? How does that separate out those who like this form of humor from those who do not? As usual, the most primitive forms of expression are, generally, the hardest to articulate and sometimes the most difficult to understand. We can say, though, that aggressive physical humor is enjoyed by aggressive, physical people. In fact, this is probably revealed most by the distaste many people have for this form of humor. What are they distasting? Perhaps it is the physical and the aggressive—that form of immediate being that we see in humans but often would rather not see; that we can enjoy physical, aggressive victories for victory's sake. "What you had is now mine." One study conducted by Dozois, Martin, and Faulkner (2013) examined the relationship between aggressive forms of humor and early psychopathology, finding that aggressive humor may be used as a maladaptive coping strategy.

We can, alternatively, enter into a compensatory view of the function of aggressive humor if we adopt the Freudian point of view (Freud, 1960). In this view, the person who is unable to express their aggressive drive would be likely to enjoy and engage in aggressive humor. The aggressive humor acts as a form of distraction in which the viewer isn't fully attentive to the fact that the humorous act is expressing aggressive compulsions (Gollob & Levine, 1967). Thus, the humor acts as a tension-reducer and produces psychological relief of such tension. There is some merit to this view. In fact, phenomenologically, the experience of humor is that of a "relief" and even of a "release" of tension of a certain sort. The aggressive humor reaction could, in fact, be aptly described in those terms. The person bursts out with a release (laughter), which is sometimes accompanied by or, soon after, followed by a sense of guilt and a kind of sly smile or expressions like, "Oh, that is so bad. That is really bad," while a revealing smile or giggle is still present.

But the difficulties with the Freudian perspective come into play when we state the hypothesis that it is precisely those who are repressed in their expression of aggression who would enjoy aggressive humor. This would imply that the simply "aggressive person" would take no joy in such aggressive comedic mediums—but we know that this is not the case. Aggressive people enjoy aggressive humor, just like sarcastic people enjoy sarcasm, for the most part.

To gain more clarity about the nature of such people who enjoy physical humor, it is necessary to recall the essence of physical humor. Most important, this type of humor relies on the physical as "the real," metaphysically. We laugh at the stuffy professor slipping on the banana peel because his physicality is real—perhaps more so than his illusions of being high society or "simply an intellect." Physical people, then, are apt to enjoy physical humor. This is, then, consistent with literature that shows, for example, that psychopaths respond more quickly and more prominently to hostile cartoons (Holmes, 1969), which is inconsistent with psychoanalytic predictions. One may also refer to the previously cited study of Dozois et al. (2013) for further exploration. Physical people revel in the physical shown to be the real, over and above the mental. This, too, helps to explain why many who do not enjoy physical humor also do not like the fact that others *do* enjoy it. There is something metaphysical at stake here. If the physical is real, they are defeated. Going back to the enjoyment that the caveman experienced upon hitting the other caveman over the head and stealing his woman—he enjoyed the physical triumphing over everything else. "I'm stronger than you, and therefore I win." Of course, if this attitude is adopted by many people, we have a society that is appalling to most of us.

What is that caveman experiencing as he tastes victory over his rival? Yes, it is a kind of release, a form of transcendence (though, one might argue, one of the lowest human forms possible). The victory is a victory over the *tyranny* of the "other" as one who stands over him. And it is this victory that is celebrated in his laughter. In that moment of victory, moreover, *the physical triumphs*; physicality is the real and everything else is pretense, unreal, and secondary. It is as much an expression of physical, not mental, as "me, not you"—but, of course, it is both.

How, then, do movies or shows such as *Jackass* participate in this primitive form of aggressive humor? Despite its rather primitive nature, the situation is a bit more complex than one might imagine. Many of the scenes involve a kind of self-destruction. Some willingly and some inadvertently submit themselves to various physical tortures while a group of others laugh hysterically at their plight. The audience member is, obviously, induced to enjoy the laughter along with the laughers. But they may be relating to the subject who is submitting to the aggression rather than the aggressor. Similarly, in regard to politics, it was found by Bippus (2007) that during political debates, self-deprecating humor (humor directed toward oneself) was found to be a more effective strategy and creates more attraction from the audience than aggressive humor (directed toward the opposing candidate).

What are people laughing at, though, in the *Jackass* movies, for example? To some extent, this is just a celebration of the bizarre and the freakish—somewhat akin to the old carnival. In fact, it would be easy to say that movies and shows like *Jackass* are the modern version of the carnival, which has largely faded as an entertainment medium. The physical freak, in fact, is featured in many of the scenes.

Perhaps lending more support to the basic or primitive nature of physical humor is research examining physical humor in primates. We do know that primates engage in a good deal of *laughter*. Most of that laughter is centered on free play and tickling—physical forms of humor. Another interesting note about humor in primates is its social nature (Davila-Ross, M., et al., 2011). Primates respond to each other's laughter with more laughter. Of course, this social component also plays a large part in human laughter.

We have, thus far, neglected the obvious in our phenomeno-logical approach to physical humor—and that is, this humor is a *celebration of the physical.* The victory of the underdog just described, for example, is also simultaneously a victory of the physical over the mental. The authorities may be in control; you are simply a janitor, no more—but the physical is the great leveler. What the appreciator of physical humor is "saying" is that the physical is a reality that cannot be denied. It is akin to that popular saying, "Even the king or the president must put his pants on one leg at a time." The unjustified authorities are, somehow, in control but, in the moment of Chaplin's wizardry, are recognized as equal in that they can still trip and fall and/or be knocked to the ground by a bumbling, innocent fool. Physical humor celebrates this equality. The physical simply cannot be denied its status as real.

Chapter 2

IMITATION AS HUMOR

Another rather immediate and direct form of humor is that of "imitation." During recess on the school grounds, a talented student impressionist imitates their stuffy, difficult teacher as the other students roll on the ground with laughter. A young child tries to speak "adult talk," and it is so funny that a YouTube video goes "viral"—and everyone must see this little kid acting as an adult. Parents get together and tell stories of their children's antics, imitating the voice of their 4-year-old, which leads to more of such stories and a lot of chuckles. Why is the pure act of imitation such a powerful form of humor? According to Duffy and Teruggi (2013), the use of imitation humor (through late-night comedy shows such as *Saturday Night Live* or *The Late Show with Stephen Colbert*) has become even more prominent in the modern era than ever before. The proliferation of such shows speaks to that observation quite clearly. If President Trump (or now, Biden) issues a statement about immigration, it is hardly humorous—but when that same statement is mocked by Alec Baldwin on *Saturday Night Live*, it cracks us up. Impersonations, such as those by Frank Caliendo of George W. Bush, are funny because they capture the idiosyncrasies of the targeted person.

Frank Caliendo (2006) begins his impersonation of George W. Bush by saying, "He is the only person I know that looks like he's always looking at the sun." He then does the Bush squint in a perfectly imitative fashion. "Can somebody do me a favor and hand me a pair of sunglasses?" His dumbing-down of George W. is very engaging. The audience can't get enough of it.

Duffy and Teruggi refer to a skit done on *Saturday Night Live* (NBC, 2008) in which Tina Fey takes on the character of Sarah Palin through physical behaviors or characteristics, such as shifting her eyes skyward while smiling. "Sarah Palin" is then asked about deregulation, in response to which she refers to her "track record" while discussing taxes. According to the authors, this play on words is humorous, as Palin, at the time, was considered by many in the nation's capital to be an outsider and a new player in the political world. Therefore, as Tina Fey imitates Sarah Palin by using the term "track record," the audience was forced to question Sarah Palin's authenticity. Duffy and Teruggi argue that simple imitation can, therefore, be a powerful force in shaping the opinions of the audience.

Van Zoonen (2005) states that political imitative humor provides a shortcut for comedians to influence. Mimicry is direct, immediate, and quite superficial but, through humor, can allow the perceiver to see the target as "inside of" some arbitrary way of seeing or being. What is the appeal of impersonation? Of course, the obvious enticement is the "taking down" of an authority, like the president. Authority figures have power over us—or at least they are supposed to. As we experience the impersonation, that power is weakened; the authority *no longer has authority* over us. The impersonator shows that the target (one who is impersonated) is not unique; instead, he can be "played" by another. He's a style or a form that can be copied.

How Serious Imitation Really Is

Another clue about the power of impersonation is the seriousness with which we prosecute the crime of "impersonating an officer" or "identity theft." These are among our worst fears—that someone could pretend to be another, especially when it's *you*, and get away with it. But when imitation is performed, done for pure humor, and one is not the target, it can be uproariously funny. After an encounter that a group of teenagers had with a policeman, one of those teenagers may conduct an impersonation of the officer with whom they interacted, to the delight of the rest of the group. "What are you doing standing in front of that store? What are your names? Do your parents know you are out here at nine p.m.?" The exaggerated tone of "seriousness" in the impersonation is largely what provides the humor.

Identity theft is a serious crime, of course, but the psychological implications of impersonation go beyond the practical consequences and literal implications of such acts. We assume that we have possession over our identities, our personhood, and the transgression of assuming that identity by another is appalling. Being subject to an impersonation is belittling and destructive because it violates that very assumption of the possession of personhood. "Can you imagine that he just started using my credit card and presented himself on an airplane as me? The gall of such a person!" This would constitute a very direct and personal insult.

Besides the debunking of an authority figure, though, what does imitation accomplish for us? How, for example, does imitation become so humorous? Why is the simple act of pretending to be another such a prominent form of comedy, such that there are professional impressionists on the comedy scene? Our first response must be that the process we're referring to is not quite as simple as it may seem. There are aspects of the target and the impressionist that must exist in order for humor to occur. For example, some targets are simply not humorous ones. Many impressionists, for example, struggled to get laughs with Obama impressions. G. W. Bush, on the other hand, and certainly Trump were powerful targets that provided strong reactions from audiences for impressionists.

What, then, are the most prominent features that lead to successful imitative humor?

Not surprisingly, we find that authority figures are, once again, prominent players (as targets) in this form of humor, as they are for so much of comedic action. The authority figure that is rigid, stuffy, and one-dimensional is the ripest of targets. Imitation is, moreover, often coupled with cynicism about the authority figure. Duffy and Teruggi conceptualize this as a "rhetorical vision" that is comprised of an insider pitted against an outsider. For example, in the case of the student impersonating his teacher, the student and the friends around him would be considered "insiders," while the teacher would be considered the "outsider." In the case of the skit done by Tina Fey, Sarah Palin was depicted as an "outsider" of Washington.

> President Reagan, being asked about deals made with the Iran Contras, sits at his presidential desk, staring into space. He then replies, "I just don't recall." He would repeat either this phrase or "I can't remember" a total of 88 times in his testimony about the Iran Contra affair. (Ryan, 2004)

One of the best examples of this was when our president, Ronald Reagan, claimed he simply could not remember many of the details of the Iran Contra transactions. For a president to not recall important details is itself somewhat humorous (as long as there are no serious consequences for the country). This was, however, especially so for Reagan—because he displayed a kind of self-righteous confidence in his public persona. The talk show hosts and impersonators had a "field day" imitating Reagan, the president, repeatedly claiming that, "I just don't recall." It was, perhaps, Reagan's persona that was being laughed at (granted, more by Democrats than Republicans) and not the issue at hand. Of course, his critics used this incidence of Reagan's appearing "clueless" and generalized it to many important issues. They both criticized and laughed at his inability to remember. Interestingly enough, hindsight now affords us the perspective that this failure to recall may have been part of a developing case of Alzheimer's disease; if we had that perspective at the time, his insistence that he could not recall details would never have been viewed as humorous.

Is imitation, then, simply another case of taking down the boss, the president, the reigning authority in a class battle in which the lower classes are allowed to triumph—in humor—in a way that they cannot in life? Are they simply allowed to experience what it feels like to be an insider rather than an outsider? Imitation humor, though, is not limited to humor in which the authority is mimicked. Think, for example, of the scapegoated child who is quirky and awkward, suffering from tics or tremors and struggling with their social world. Are they not often the target of imitation, by the strong, popular in-group? Why would an in-group feel the need to make fun of and triumph over those that they already dominate?

Ferguson and Ford (2008) address this "disparagement humor" and how it relates to superiority theory. According to the authors, this type of humor is targeted to amuse through the use of denigration or derogation of a target. In a classic study by Middleton (1959), in-group disparagement humor was found to be humorous only when the target does not identify with the in-group. For example, black participants found anti-white jokes more humorous than white participants did.

Imitation may be one of the oldest forms of humor. One striking aspect of this form of humor, though, is that it is an inherently *social* form of humor. There would literally be no value in simply imitating another without an audience. The imitative act also is contagious or addictive; once the impressionist gets started, others may be inspired to try their hand at an imitation or to coax the expert impressionist for more and more impersonations. "Can you do President Trump? How about Jack Nicholson?" The audience never seems fully saturated as the impressionist portrays celebrity after celebrity. It is as if the delight is a *state of mind* that has motivational power; it seeks to be continued or even exaggerated as the impersonator begins to exaggerate or accentuate his impersonations.

What, then, is in the delight that we feel upon watching an impersonation? It is, indeed, a form of domination or victory over the other as we make fun of him through imitation. Much like other forms of imitative humor, disparagement humor is found most amusing by those whose identity (either personal or social) is heightened in a specific social context. This concept relates specifically to the insider/outsider dynamic mentioned earlier, in which the target suddenly becomes the outsider and the imitator becomes the insider within a particular social context. If one can be replicated, then one has inherently lost one's status as the source or creator of themselves. The once formidable other is reduced to a *form* that is replicable by the other; their uniqueness and originality is, thus, diminished or defeated.

I can be me, or I can be you—that is what is being "said" by the impersonator—and, therefore, I am certainly superior to you. In the early 1970s, several studies (La Fave, 1972; La Fave, et al., 1973; & La Fave et al., 1974) were conducted that demonstrated the increase of self-esteem that occurs as a result of disparagement humor that targets a *negative identification class*. But is this actually a form of superiority?

Rather than use the term "superior," I would prefer "transcendent" because what is meant here by impersonation is that the target is not unique and unclassifiable—and that there is a freedom of movement between persons. One is not completely unique or, we might say, a free subject—if others can imitate that person. One is a form or object that can be "captured" by others. That reduction to form is, also, precisely what allows for transcendence for the audience. If the president is "reduced to form," then his power as president over you is no longer; you are transcendent over him, even though he is the president.

Baldwin as Trump: Powerful Imitative Humor

In the case of a president who was viewed by many as truly oppressive, such as Donald Trump, imitation provided a kind of relief that was so powerful some have remarked, "I can't live without Alec Baldwin's skits that make fun of Trump." Indeed, Baldwin's portrayal has taken off worldwide. What provides such relief for those who feel that Trump is oppressing them?

Baldwin immediately appears in a mocking mode. He is at the White House, in a very legitimate setting for a U.S. president. He has all of the appropriate clothes, demeanor, and attitude of the president. But as the audience looks at the expression on "Trump's" face, they experience immediate relief. The face of Baldwin's Trump is vacuous, a caricature of Trump's actual "look." He states his opinions impulsively and without regard for consequences. There is no "true thought" behind his face, yet at the same time, it is clearly very much Donald Trump. The depiction of Trump is, granted, a caricature of who he really is, but there are enough relevant examples, allusions, and concepts that make the portrayal very applicable to the current situation at hand. In fact, since he is at once an extreme caricature of the person himself and also very realistically portrayed (mainly focusing on hand gestures and facial expressions), one is torn. The audience knows that the humor is ridiculous and silly—but they're "taken in" by it, nonetheless.

Let's return to the question of the "relief" such humor provides: We can notice the moment of imitative humor as distinctly providing transcendent relief. In ordinary life, the president appears as an authority whose rules, plans, and thoughts are viewed as inhibiting, condescending, and marginalizing to a large portion of society. When Baldwin is "in character," though, we are allowed to experience the ridiculous arbitrariness and absurdity of Trump as recognizable and revealed as what they are, in the plain light of day (though late at night on a Saturday, of course). It is as if those features of Trump's personality are laid bare in a way that they become openly seen. The biases that are revealed, moreover, appear foolish, one-sided, and without merit. That is the point where Trump (the actual person) usually terminated his appearances or press conferences, trying to save face. In watching the Baldwin impersonation, though, we're allowed to see Trump in his most irrational, tyrannical, and narcissistic mode. That provided a great relief for the largely Democratic audience.

Imitation of the Serious Person

There is another kernel present in imitation that should not be overlooked. This is the seriousness of the target as the source of humor. The most hilarious impersonations are of *very serious people*, acting very seriously. It is this moment where the target being imitated is most "inside of" themselves that is captured by the impersonation. We are their outside. They are inside themselves. We see them as form, as only an "inside of" that they cannot extricate themselves from. But the impersonator acts as a medium to allow us to no longer be subject to the seriousness since they are not even the source of what they are saying. The medium lays bare the essence of that form in gestures and mannerisms; they are "captured" by the impersonator. The audience member, then, is able to digest the serious person at this point. It is as if they are a steak cut up into many manageable pieces. They are no longer whole and can no longer be taken *seriously* since they are seen as form, not person.

The serious person serves as the best target for impersonation, much like the stuffy, overly serious person was mocked in Chaplin's silent movies. The one who takes themselves seriously, as if they are unique and powerful, becomes the prime target. What is shown in the impersonation, then, is that they are neither unique nor powerful. That relief is experienced as humor and manifest in laughter. Leibovich (2008) described the importance of Tina Fey's *Saturday Night Live* impersonations of Sarah Palin. According to Leibovich, those successive *Saturday Night Live* skits were influential in the 2008 election campaigns because Palin (someone who took herself seriously politically) was intimately linked with Tina Fey (someone who was not to be taken seriously). Palin's power was diminished as she was portrayed as unsophisticated and inexperienced by Fey. Of course, one could argue that the portrayal was deserved or earned by Palin, depending upon your perspective. But the connection that Fey made with Palin's persona was, indeed, hard to shake and probably played a significant role in the election.

Most likely, then, it is not simply the seriousness of the target that is reduced in humor and experienced as relief. The *authority* of the person in question is also diminished or negated in the humorous moment. If they are neither unique nor powerful, we are relieved of the authority that they wield as superior. Humor, again, is the great equalizer that allows for the power of the other to be overcome. Transcendence of authority rules at that moment.

Imitation of the Scapegoat

Have you seen Ken when he gets excited about something in class? He's like huffing and puffing, raising his hand like this (making an imitative gesture) like he has to take a shit—badly. Then, when he's not called on, it gets even worse (exaggerating the gesture). Finally, he gives up (shows frustrated gesture) and throws a temper tantrum (thrusting his hands up and down on the desk). Onlookers increasingly laugh with each imitation. (fictional vignette)

What can we say about the imitation of an oppressed person or the *scapegoat* who is imitated? Why would there be a need to overcome or dominate one who is already "down and out" or even helpless? Watson (2011) describes imitative humor of those who are superior as "joking up," while imitative humor of those who are inferior is described as "joking down." Of course, we should immediately take note that there is a dividing line here. Some will reject such humor and refuse to partake in it. They view such denigration of the weak or physically challenged as evil and intolerable. They may even utter the simple statement that, "That is just not funny. Stop that!" when others may, for example, impersonate a person who suffers from cerebral palsy. In fact, this form of humor is usually engaged in with a safe group of friends or family where the risk of criticism is minimal—because it is, indeed, a sinful pleasure if one at all.

Ziv (2010) points to the fact that humor, in general, is a way to strengthen bonds between group members. The research conducted by Ziv suggests that the humor and laughter involved in denigrating the scapegoat can provide feelings of pleasure within that group, leading to further cohesion and preservation of consensus. One can see how the imitation of the oppressed might further increase this cohesion, as the humor in question is socially taboo but accepted within the group. Most of the time, the indulgers know that this type of laughter is "wrong" and not politically or even morally acceptable.

We cannot, however, dismiss the fact that some will partake in such humor, which leads us to the question of what is accomplished by virtue of such imitation. First and foremost, people who have obvious weaknesses demand our empathy. We would like to think that life is free and easy and that others do not require our help. Those who have physical or mental disabilities remind us that this is not the case. By externalizing that negative reality in making fun of the weaker person, we are able to maintain our belief in the free and easy life we seek. Perhaps even more important, we gain distance from the reality that we could be subject to the kind of suffering they are enduring.

Also, though they are weak and perhaps, helpless, the scapegoated person still may cause trouble or be *high maintenance* for others. They may even, through their weakness, ask for help from others, either explicitly or implicitly. By imitating them, we portray them as weak and pitiful, and no further claims or demands can be made on us with regard to them. They can make no such claims because they are laughable, ridiculous, and pathetic. In the imitation, of course, their disabilities are made more explicit and more dramatic. Their walk is even shakier, their movements jerkier, and their speech more drooling and sillier. By laughing at them, we assert a kind of dominance over them, which frees us of our responsibility and empathy for them—and all that they represent about the truth about life.

What we are *gaining*, though, is not so much transcendence over the person themselves, because this type of humor is rarely experienced in the presence of the imitated scapegoat. This, in fact, serves as a clue that the value of this humor is in the overcoming of one's own unrecognized tendency toward empathy in relation to the scapegoated. Watson (2011) provides an example in discussing the use of "gallows humor" in medicine. According to Watson, gallows humor is experienced when medical professionals joke about their patients' problems.

It was 3:00 a.m. and three tired emergency room residents were wondering why the pizza they'd ordered hadn't come yet. A nurse interrupted their pizza complaints with a shout: "GSW Trauma One—no pulse, no blood pressure." The residents rushed to meet the gurney and immediately recognized the unconscious shooting victim: he was the teenage delivery boy from their favorite all-night restaurant, and he'd been mugged bringing their dinner. That made them work even harder. A surgeon cracked the kid's rib cage and exposed his heart, but the bullet had torn it open and they couldn't even stabilize him for the OR. After forty minutes of resuscitation, they called it: time of death, 4:00 a.m. The young doctors shuffled into the temporarily empty waiting area. They sat in silence. Then David said what all three were thinking: "What happened to our pizza?" Joe found their pizza box where the delivery boy had dropped it before he ran from his attackers. It was face up, a few steps away from the ER's sliding doors. Joe set it on the table. They stared at it. Then one of the residents made a joke: "How much do you think we ought to tip him?" The residents laughed. Then they ate the pizza. (Watson, 2011, p. 37).

Watson theorizes that gallows humor allowed the physicians to see the patient as less than a patient, relieving them of the guilt involved in their failure to successfully treat the patient. The burden of caring for the other—which is an obvious consequence of their profession—is thus reduced or obliterated in the humorous act. It unites the group in a way that many may see as sinister. Watson claims, however, that when problems are beyond our control (such as the inevitability of death in the previous example), the laughter that accompanies gallows humor can be a relatively adaptive method of coping.

Parody As Imitation

Another aspect of imitative humor is that of parody. Parody is defined as a "literary or musical work in which the style of an author or work is closely imitated for comic effect or in ridicule" (*Merriam-Webster*, 2020). The art involved in parody is that ability to imitate but *exaggerate one key aspect* of the ridiculed target. Mel Brooks is truly a master of parody. In *History of the World: Part I* (Brooks, et al., 1981), he creates a complete dance scene out of the Spanish Inquisition. The Grand Inquisitor, played by Brooks himself, is a kind of nightclub dance star who orchestrates a musical number that is focused on the Spanish Inquisition. The contrast between a lively, celebratory show tune dance scene and the darkness of the Inquisition is what triggers the comedic.

In *Blazing Saddles* (Hertzberg & Brooks, 1974), Brooks turns his attention to the American Western form of film. All the elements of Westerns are present—cowboys, "Indians," battles, loyalty issues, chases, and cheesy romances. What Brooks does, however, is make a mockery of this form of entertainment by exaggerating all these aspects in a way that casts them as absurd or at least frivolous. The romances are overly dramatic, the battles are fought over nothing, and both cowboys and "Indians" are depicted as caricatures of their usual selves. It is as if the form is emptied of its content, so it stands revealed and easily seen for what is—a macho but shallow narrative. But there is another dimension to Brooks's humor that cannot be overlooked, and that is the love for the form that he is, at the same time, ridiculing in his work. The silliness of the gestures that are portrayed in *Blazing Saddles* only serve to underscore the beauty and wonder of the form because it holds up even under the greatest scrutiny or exposure. To this day, Brooks remains a great lover of American Westerns.

What is the *mechanism* by which parody is enjoyed? Again, a kind of relief is part of the equation. It is as if the pressure of having to take Westerns seriously is suddenly removed and one can see the Western as truly juvenile and foolish. Parody allows us to finally laugh at those elements without restriction. One rule of thumb in comedy seems to be that the more serious the target of humor, the more humorous the outcome. Think again of the targets used by Chaplin in his physical humor—stuffy, pompous, stiff men who took themselves too seriously.

Parody can also be activated by forms of art we find uncomfortable or challenging. Creekmur (2007) analyzes the parodies that emerged around the film *Brokeback Mountain* (2005). The author discusses the various parodies that stemmed from the movie, and links this to the fact that the movie is basically vacant in terms of humor. Because homosexuality causes many people discomfort, it is not surprising that so many parodies arose from *Brokeback Mountain* as a way of releasing the tension experienced by many viewers who were uncomfortable with the very open homosexuality in the film.

Yet we see that parody (as with nearly all imitative humor), at the same time, actually reveals the validity, at least aesthetically, of the art form in question. It may use poetry to expose poetry, sarcasm to expose hypocrisy, or mockery to expose fakery, but, at the same time, it therefore demonstrates the power of that format to provide entertainment. For example, it is quite possible that those who appreciate *Blazing Saddles* the most, in fact, are lovers of the Western modality of film. In the end, parody induces a kind of transcendence by propelling us beyond the art form in question while truly loving and respecting that art form at the same time.

People Who Enjoy Imitative Humor

The fact that the audience member is able to "participate" in this mocking in a vicarious way makes it, perhaps, particularly satisfying. No sacrifice is required by the audience member, after all. They are allowed to simply witness the impersonation and gain the benefits that it entails. The delight, moreover, seems to depend upon the degree to which the impersonator has accurately "captured" the target. "That's just like him—the way you raised your eyebrows and twisted your face that way!" exclaims the audience member. In fact, this form of humor, because of its rather primitive nature, will carry some aspects of the sort of humor that we will, later, discuss under the heading of the "hilariously funny." It is *immediate and moving* in the moment, unlike, for example, a joke that can be repeated and told. "You wouldn't believe how John is able to impersonate Larry—you have to see it! I was dying of laughter!"

Often, it is a person who possesses a form of irreverence but lacks the capacity to carry out or express that rebellion who would most profit from watching impersonation. Again, this is a very effortless form of humor, requiring little interpretation. Imitative humor may also be used to impress or entertain a potential lover or friend. This is what Martin (2007) calls "affiliative humor," which is designed to endear others to you and provide greater ease in social interactions.

> "Good morning, class. Today we will have a pop quiz. If you haven't been keeping up with the reading, good luck. You might as well just turn in your paper blank because this is all based on the really awful reading that probably nobody has done. You young people do not appreciate James Joyce and now you're going to pay the price for that." Included in the impersonation, of course, are all the facial gestures and verbal intonations, which are grossly exaggerated by the student impersonating the teacher. (fictional vignette)

A person may perform this impersonation of their teacher after school to the delight of their classmates. What do they get out of it? How do each of them benefit? The impersonator is able to supersede the authority of the teacher and place themselves in the realm of "top dog" in relation to their classmates. The audience of classmates are passive witnesses who are able to enjoy the irreverent mocking of the teacher. Perhaps they are good, wholesome students who obey all of the teacher's orders and have been completing all the assigned readings. At some level, however, they might realize that the teacher is a bit absurd, sadistic, and pathetic. They are able to enjoy the irreverence of the impersonator without any negative social implications.

Shared laughter can help to unite and increase pleasure within a group setting, as well. Along with this pleasure comes bonding within the group and possibly attraction to the impersonator who is providing the humor and subsequent laughter. Ziv (2010) states that humor, in general, helps to determine mutual suitability between people, which may lead to mutual attraction between potential lovers or groups of friends.

In some ways, imitative humor is at the core of all humor. We have—with, hopefully, no derogation intended—referred to it as *primitive* because of its directness and immediacy. On the other hand, imitative humor clearly is *symbolic* since the action in the imitation lives in fantasy, not real-time action, if you will. The imitator is reflecting on experience, not living real experience, at the moment of their imitation. As one imitates another, moreover, they are getting "outside" the person in question—which we will continue to argue is at the core of a great deal of humor. The transcendence that occurs as the audience enjoys imitative humor is very powerful. What the impersonator is saying is, essentially, "I can be you."

The "I can be you" gesture, on the other hand, can be a devastating one for the imitated person. At the school where I taught, the psychology department engaged in an annual ritual for a while where the students would perform some imitative skits at the end of the year, playing the roles of the psychology professors. Some of the professors were appalled at the first instantiation of this and demanded that they not be included in subsequent iterations of this event. If another can "capture" the person in question, then that other is no longer unique and is not outside the range of other people's being. Keep in mind that the opposite of imitative humor is "taking the other seriously." One cannot take the target of imitation seriously any longer. This is why the imitation of the professors was met with riotous laughter and joy, especially from the other students, but some professors found it extremely painful.

A great relief is found when the other is no longer other but, instead, a form or style that can be tried on, grasped, or captured. When an oppressive president, for example, is imitated, those who are suffering at the hands of that president often find immediate relief in that imitative humor. They transcend, for the moment, since the authority of that president is *no longer real* and is, therefore, rendered impotent. Of course, this relief is fleeting and quite limited in that, soon, order is restored and one is still subject to that president. But again, once imitated, some of the power of that oppressive president is reduced for the observer, and they can reinvoke that moment by discussing this in conversation—e.g., "Did you see that impersonator do Trump last night? Oh, it was hilarious!"

This is, of course, the limitation of imitative humor—that it needs to be continually reinvoked and reinvented. The imitated target can and will return to their serious position after a time, which is usually quite short. Therefore, the "class clown" who imitates the teacher must do so on a regular basis. Their original mock does not stand. An audience is needed, and the moment repeated, over and over—because this form of humor simply does not carry any enduring power.

So, what type of person is attracted to imitative humor? One who has an implicit criticism of others that cannot be explicitly expressed. The impersonator, then, allows that person to experience a form of transcendence that they cannot bring into existence themselves or articulate; it is done for them by the impersonator. By watching the impersonator, the person is able to experience that critique from a transcendent distance while still maintaining their social dignity. There may also be an ambivalence about laughing at another, which appears as a "sinful pleasure" type of experience— one they are not proud of but cannot resist.

Chapter 3

OBSERVATIONAL HUMOR

Do you ever get lip crud? That crud on your lip? It's kind of a sticky film, a gooey coating? You know, if it dries a bit, it's kind of a gummy, cruddy, flaky, crusty kind of thing. It starts in the corner of your mouth and works its way down your lip. And if it's really bad, the corners of your mouth look like parentheses? Do you ever have that? (Carlin, 2001)

This is an excerpt from a George Carlin routine that is focused on weird stuff about our bodies that we never talk about. This form of humor is striking because it is difficult to determine what the "comic" aspect is. There does not seem to be a punchline; there is no contrast that is pointed out, no narrative, and no political commentary. Many of the aspects we see in other forms of humor are strikingly absent from observational humor. Upon reflection, it is clear that the simple "observation" is precisely what is humorous. But what does this "observation" accomplish for us? How is it funny to point out small details of life?

One beginning point here is to examine the contrast between public and private life that this form of humor highlights. Lip crud is something everyone has noticed but has probably never discussed in public. The comic violates that unwritten rule that you do not talk about private matters and bodily functions in a public setting. The private, therefore, becomes public. There is a sheepish, revelatory laughter that this form of humor triggers. Laughter ensues at the recognition of the way this private aspect of life is readily recognizable, able to be articulated, and can be shared with others, while a taboo exists against its being publicly discussed.

> A lot of couples shower together. It's supposed to be romantic and sensual. Truth? It's not all it's cracked up to be. Because one of you is not getting water. One of you, therefore, is not taking a shower. (Reiser, 1994, p.161)

> Kissing is a wonderful thing, but there's an inherent design flaw: I don't think anyone's face is supposed to be that close to your face for that length of time. It's just odd. If for no other reason, it's frightening. Why do you think people close their eyes when they kiss? Think about it. In the real world, if you saw someone an inch and a half away, coming at you with their eyes open and their lips puckered, you'd scream. It's alarming. (Reiser, 1994, p. 277)

These observations, from Paul Reiser's book *Couplehood*, point out aspects of experience that we are, at some level, aware of but generally push away from consciousness. In the first example, we romanticize a shared shower as sensual and romantic, but, in actual experience, it is, as he says, a bit difficult because only one person can stand under the showerhead at a time. The other person is a bit cold and uncomfortable. Why is pointing that out actually funny, though? Once again, observational humor seems to play on our level of awareness. It points to content that we can recognize but have never allowed ourselves to formulate or articulate. Let's say that we know that romantic showers are not really as good as they are cracked up to be, but we maintain the delusion that they are wonderful. Reiser, as the comic, points out this contrast. At that point, we are unable to maintain the delusion and are forced to recognize the truth. It's that contrast, that moment of recognition of the truth, that makes us laugh. It's a laugh of a kind of embarrassment for having held on to an untenable belief—which is now impossible to maintain.

> My wife and I were intellectuals—before we had kids.
>
> Everyone says that kids are pure and innocent. That's not true; they're liars!
>
> I am not the boss in my family. I'm not sure how I lost it. I'm not sure when I lost it. I don't know if I ever had it. (Cosby, 1982)

Bill Cosby was one of the great observational humorists. Of course, his character has certainly fallen into disrepute—but we will leave that aside for the moment. One of his most hilarious routines invokes his experience at the dentist. He provides vivid examples of the whole process of being worked on at the dentist, with all the features that are usually present in the experience. It is a common experience that Cosby brings to life in his dramatic presentation. Probably the funniest aspect of this routine is Cosby's depiction of the patient who is trying to communicate with the dentist while his mouth is filled with the dentist's pokers and other instruments. What is striking, and common, here is that the dentist continues to ask questions of the patient while the patient is not able to respond in an understandable way, given the dental instruments that are in his mouth.

But there is a mystery here in observational humor that must be addressed. How is the depiction of the *commonplace* so intriguing, exciting, and humorous? Several factors play into this. First, the experience at the dentist is not something that people generally talk about at length. It's a common but somewhat private experience. There is a kind of personal embarrassment about the inside of one's mouth that leads to a *protective* approach to the dental experience. One might discuss it with family but not friends, for example. Cosby is, therefore, violating a social norm simply by entering into a full-scale depiction of the dental chair. The dental pain may also play a role in the humor here. While "in" the experience, one is often in pain, but when listening to the comedian, the freedom from pain allows for one to get "outside" the experience itself, and this facilitates the humorous moment.

This leads to an even more central aspect of observational humor: Observational humor, generally, allows for a form of *transcendence*. At the moment of recognition, we are no longer subject to the experience itself. For example, the experience of being in the dental chair is one where we are a helpless *subject*. We're subject to the other—the world, the state of our own teeth—and have little power or control. The humorous moment, then, brings a kind of freedom that the comic has released in us. We now share the experience with others, are "looking at it," and are no longer helplessly subject to it. Observational humor, then, has as its aim a kind of transcendence that accompanies being *outside* that which one observes.

> "Are you one of those comedians that does that 'Did you ever notice' type of stuff?"
>
> "Yes."
>
> "Oh, I don't really like that kind of humor."

This bit from a *Seinfeld* episode is interesting because it moves in the direction of demeaning or diminishing observational humor by providing still another eye, a meta-level that would oversee this whole form of humor and render it limited or even impotent. The observational humorist relies on the moment of transcendence that they provide as the decisive moment. When they ask, "Did you ever notice . . . ?" they invite the audience member to participate in a naïve experience of appreciating observational humor. If the whole enterprise is grasped *as an enterprise*, then the tables are turned. The audience member is now "the knower," the transcendent one, and the comedian is looked at as "inside" of a certain (limited) form of humor. Interestingly, though, by being the writer of the comedy bit, Seinfeld manages to one-up the critic by laughing at the whole scene from the standpoint of a knowing observer. The audience of the show, moreover, knowing that Seinfeld is the author of the bit is forced to recognize that Seinfeld is not simply "caught up" in a form of humor but transcendent to it, as well.

Observing Craziness in the Other

> When Needleman was staying at my house as a guest, I knew he liked a particular brand of tuna fish. I stocked the guest kitchen with it. He was too shy to admit his fondness for it to me, but once, thinking he was alone, opened every can and mused, "You are all my children."
>
> Scotland, 1823: A man has been arrested for stealing a crust of bread. "I only like the crust," he explains, and he is identified as the thief who has recently terrorized several chophouses by stealing just the end cut of roast beef.
>
> He frequently would forget to remove the coat hanger from his jacket while he wore it. A colleague reminded him of it one time at a Princeton Commencement and he smiled calmly and said, "Good, let those who have taken issue with my theories think at least that I have broad shoulders." (Allen, 1986)

The playful, silly humor of Woody Allen here is directly looking at the other's behavior and seeing it as crazy, irrational, and even absurd. He takes basic human needs, such as the need to appear strong, and demonstrates how we will go to extreme measures (e.g., wearing the hanger of a jacket to appear to have broad shoulders) to satisfy those needs. In the first two examples given here, Allen focuses on the other's quirky habits or even fetishes—one for a particular brand of tuna fish and another for the ends of bread and roast beef. The reader or audience is then allowed to laugh at just how quirky and bizarre a person can be.

Note that, in each case, the target of the humor is a *serious person* engaged in, for them, weighty issues. It is that seriousness that triggers our laughter. The one who has a fetish for bread crusts or a certain brand of tuna fish is, apparently, as described, dead serious about that interest. In the case of the tuna fish, he waits until he feels he is alone and then declares that "You are all my children." But it is precisely the target's seriousness that allows for the humor to emerge; one simply *cannot* or at least *should not* be that serious about tuna fish! But, somehow, this man is, which we find hilarious.

In this category of comedy—laughing at the irrational—we have another form of "laughing at," which is clearly an amoral form of transcendence of the other. "Did you hear what the principal said yesterday at school?" the schoolboy exclaims. "No more short shorts allowed in school. They'll be measuring everyone's shorts from now on." His audience is, then, able to laugh at the irrational authority in their nit-picking rules.

The middle-aged son is summoned to his father's house with urgency. His father has been suffering with moderate Alzheimer's symptoms for quite some time, so the son is apprehensive about what he may encounter as he enters the door to his family home.

Dad: "Oh, good. You're finally here. We have to get going immediately."

Son: "Why? Where do we have to go?"

Dad: "To the ballpark. We have to get to the ballpark, the game is starting."

Son: "Which ballpark?

Dad: "The Ashkenazi Stadium. You know, where the Ashkenazi Chiefs play."

Son: "Why? To see the game?"

Dad: "They called me. They need me to play!"

Son: "Are you sure? You haven't played sports in thirty years, Dad."

Dad: "Don't question it. We have to get going. They need me!"

Son: "Alright, Dad. But let me just ask you a question. What position do they want you to play?"

Dad: "Outfield. One of their outfielders was hurt."

Son: "Are you sure you're up for this, Dad?"

Dad: "Of course. Let's go."

Son: "Really? Are you sure?"

Dad: "You know, maybe it isn't such a good idea after all. It might be really hard to wheel this wheelchair out to the outfield at that field!" (Source who chose anonymity)

This story was told to me by a colleague, long after his father was deceased, but it remains one of the family's "jewel" stories. We can say that the father was "out of his mind" at the time of this incident, but that does not explicate the humor in the story here. It is the combination of his sense of importance—the urgency with which he approaches this need to go to the ballpark with his lack of "reality testing" that proves to be so funny. He's convinced of his own reality beyond a shadow of a doubt. That reality, though, when looked at by the observer, is patently absurd.

What makes this story particularly hilarious, though, is the integration of both realities in the father's final formulation. It would be too far to go to the outfield—because of the reality of the wheelchair. The presence of the wheelchair, however, is evidence that playing baseball at a competitive level is, of course, out of the question. It may be, in fact, that the father's fantasy-reality was beginning to break down under the son's questioning—such that the two realities were perfectly placed, side by side, for the observer to see. The incongruity, then, is readily apparent.

Categorization and Labeling

Much of the power of observational humor is in the language used to describe events. George Carlin's discussion of "lip crud" would probably not rise to the level of humor if not for the humorous quality of the word "crud." It's odd, funny, rare, and a bit disgusting. The specific language used in humor is, of course, no accident and is the focus of chapter five of this book.

The concept of categorization, though, which is so critical in cognitive psychology (Miller, et al., 2010), is also applied regularly in humor. Simply labeling something as such can provide humor to the receiver of that humor. Larry David, for example, has a bit in *Curb Your Enthusiasm* on the "stop and chat." When you run into a friend on the street, you often need to decide whether it's necessary or desirable to stop and chat with that friend. As David labels this as "the stop and chat," it becomes reified. Moral questions arise: Do you have to stop and chat with a casual acquaintance or not? How long does the absence have to be between two casual friends whereby a stop and chat is necessary? If you choose to not do the "stop and chat" thing and go merrily on your way, is that a serious, actionable insult to the friend?

Seinfeld and David are absolute experts on labeling and categorization (Irwin, 2000). Their famous label of "master of my own domain," for example, gained a great deal of public interest and earned a lot of laughs. The concepts of "double-dipping," being a "bad breaker-upper," "man hands," "regifting," and a "manzier" were all created by Seinfeld/David (and their writers) and produce almost immediate laughter, just in themselves. Giving a name to something that is quite familiar but never labeled may be humorous in itself. The particularities of why a name is funny is a separate question altogether. "Master of my own domain," for example, has the added benefit of having sexual content that is taboo in society, since it focuses on masturbation.

What does labeling or categorizing something actually "do" for the receiver of humor? Once again, it allows for a personal transcendence of sorts. What is labeled is that which one is beyond by virtue of placing a limited label or category on it. We've packaged it and conquered it, in a sense, by labeling it.

The discussion of the "stop and chat," which gives a label to the phenomenon and also raises some critical questions about the closeness of the social relationship between the two, allows us to enter into the question with humor. Part of the humor is "taking so seriously" something that is clearly not a terribly serious issue. Whether to stop and chat or not is not a life-or-death situation; it's inherently trivial. In a piece on *60 Minutes*, in fact, Larry David's humor was once characterized as "making the trivial seem important." Much of observational humor can be understood in this context.

Deadpan Humor

In the classic deadpan humor, a person is confronted with the completely irrational but maintains a kind of objectivity (emotionless) in the face of that irrationality. This results in the listener seeing the contradiction and provides a kind of freedom from the absurdity of what is presented. The deadpan expression of the comic facilitates this process.

Steven Wright (1985) is probably the most prominent modern-day master of deadpan humor. He uses mainly one-liners but also a series of narratives. In each case, he lacks any emotional response and appears to look curiously on at the observations he makes.

It's a small world but I wouldn't want to paint it.

For my birthday I got a humidifier and a de-humidifier. I put them in the same room and let them fight it out.

I drive way too fast to worry about cholesterol.

I spilled spot remover on my dog. Now he's gone.

I went to a general store. They wouldn't let me buy anything specifically. (Wright, 1985)

The one-liner seems perfectly suited for deadpan humor. It's quick, it's droll and dry, and it delivers a fast punch. The receiver of deadpan must be witty and fast-thinking because there is always an unexpected twist in the deadpan one-liner. This type of humor is all about *contrast*. It is the contrast involved in the unexpected twist that provides the experience of humor, essentially, but the deadpan delivery of the comic also contrasts strongly with the humor (and laughter) that the receiver might experience.

Mitch Hedberg was another excellent deadpan, one-liner specialist, whose life was cut short by a drug overdose at the age of 37. Here are some examples of his observational, deadpan humor:

I don't have a girlfriend. But I do know a woman who'd be mad at me for saying that.

I like an escalator because it cannot break. It can just become stairs.

I used to do drugs. I still do, but I used to, too.

You know, I'm sick of following my dreams, man. I'm just going to ask where they're going and hook up with 'em later.

My fake plants died because I did not pretend to water them. (Hedberg, 2020)

The bit about drugs is noteworthy because the phrase, "I used to do drugs" is so commonly used as a way of distancing oneself from a socially unacceptable form of behavior. The twist that "I still do drugs" has at least two humorous benefits—that it is unexpected and, also, that it is socially unacceptable. The third element is its frank honesty and the fact that, perhaps, many people who say that they used to take drugs may very well still do them—and what the joke reveals is that simply because you used to do drugs does not mean that you no longer engage in drug use.

People Who Enjoy Observational Humor

People who enjoy observational humor are, most likely, people who are astute observers of human behavior—and, perhaps, particularly of their own. Those who love the comedy of George Carlin, Seinfeld, Steven Wright, or even Bill Cosby see a great deal of "kernels of truth" in the observational humor they find in these formats. In the moment of revelation about the lip crud, the rules of relationships, and the trials and tribulations involved in raising children, they see themselves. The humor, though, allows for a "comic relief" from the humdrum of their everyday existence, despite the fact that the humor is generally focused on the mundane. Taboos are broken, and the receiver of this humor is able to temporarily transcend, finding relief by the expression of such realities that are usually kept beneath the surface and hidden.

We could say that a certain form of cynicism could be present in the lover of observational humor. They believe that many social mores and practices are unfounded and arbitrary. Raising questions about what conditions necessitate the "stop and chat" with a casual friend reveals that social rules and regulations are questionable, at best. They are, then, relieved that the comedian has opened up those questions and exposed the arbitrary status of the social fabric.

Chapter 4

SARCASM AND SATIRE

The real estate broker shows a young couple a house that has been on the market for some time. As they enter the house, the smell of mold is overwhelming, dead insects are scattered across the linoleum, and the floors creak as they walk on them. "We've found our dream house," exclaims the husband. (fictional narrative)

Sarcasm, as a form of humor, has received little research attention. One approach that examined sarcasm early on was the Freudian model (Freud, 1905). In this view, sarcasm was seen as a manifestation of unconscious aggression. This is a difficult point to argue—for or against. Philosophical critics of Freud, like Grunbaum (1984), would likely argue that this Freudian analysis is, at best, speculative and not falsifiable because it resorts to the existence of an unseen entity—the unconscious. But the question of causality can be debated endlessly, and, in fact, it is not the central concern here. Our task is to enter into the phenomenology of the experience of sarcasm more than speculating about its causes. The key question is, then, "What is the sarcastic person *accomplishing* in the moment of their sarcasm?"

Sarcasm is defined as, "A sharp and often satirical or ironic utterance designed to cut or give pain" or "a mode of satirical wit depending for its effect on bitter, caustic, and often ironic language that is usually directed against an individual" (*Merriam-Webster*,

2020). Sarcasm has been referred to as the lowest form of wit. This statement can be found in many places, though its origin appears to be unknown. What is meant by this is that sarcasm is, perhaps, the basest form of wit in that it is simple and yet also very negating. In fact, it is this negation that forms the "bite" in sarcasm.

Most sarcasm seems to target or refer to a positive state that is not the case. For example, following a very boring lecture, someone says, "That lecture was just so riveting!" This is not exclusive, by any means, because there are times when people watch an amazing pianist and say something like, "He needs to learn how to play the piano, doesn't he?" with sarcasm. A child who always achieves high grades brings home another 100 test score, and the mother says to the father, "She just needs to study more, obviously!" In each of these cases, there is a *reversal* of the truth. The positive is expressed in negative terms, or the negative is expressed in positive terms, for effect. If we use an inclusive definition, these sarcastic compliments also qualify—but notice that most definitions of sarcasm include the bitter, cutting aspect—which would preclude the positive-stated-negatively from being true sarcasm. The essence of sarcasm seems to be its sharp and caustic nature.

Satire is based on the same principles as sarcasm and has many of the same phenomenological properties, so it will be treated under the same umbrella here. Definitions include, "A literary work holding up human vices and follies to ridicule or scorn" and "Wit, irony, or sarcasm used to expose and discredit vice or folly." (*Merriam-Webster*, 2020). The format tends to be fairly homogeneous; political beliefs or policies are mocked by being sarcastically ridiculed. Satire often takes the form of apparent compliments that are meant to reveal the foolishness of a particular point of view or political position.

Although the term "irony" is sometimes used in reference to satire, we will see that irony is not, properly, part of satirical humor. True irony—which we will examine in chapter 12—would provide a deeper transformation that satire cannot. Satire, like sarcasm, is meant to attack and expose the other such that one finds the other's behavior foolish, resistant, or stupid. Again, satire is usually interconnected with sarcasm but in a political or decidedly social forum.

Voltaire's *Candide* (1759) is often used as a classic example of satire. At the time, a popular point of view was the kind of "empty optimism" that Voltaire found absurd. In *Candide*, the naive protagonist, despite all sorts of personal and social disasters, continually proclaims that all is for the best in this, the best of all possible worlds! Voltaire attempts to expose the absurdity of this empty optimism through the voice of Candide, who remains consistently optimistic.

Our task, though, is not to split hairs about the labeling of types of humor but to examine the nature and use of humor. What is the effect of satire or sarcasm and why would it be utilized? Why, for example, would one not simply state the truth—"That was a really boring lecture," or "Suzie is a terrific student"? The most obvious answer to that question is that the straight truth would not be humorous. Humor is built on the nonobvious, reversals, clever twists, and the unexpected. But what is gained by sarcasm, and why do some people use it so regularly whereas others hardly at all? Take a look at Michael Moore's essay on George Bush's handling of Hurricane Katrina for a document filled with satire and sarcasm.

Friday, September 2nd, 2005

Dear Mr. Bush:

Any idea where all our helicopters are? It's Day 5 of Hurricane Katrina and thousands remain stranded in New Orleans and need to be airlifted. Where on earth could you have misplaced all our military choppers? Do you need help finding them? I once lost my car in a Sears parking lot. Man, was that a drag.

Also, any idea where all our national guard soldiers are? We could really use them right now for the type of thing they signed up to do, like helping with national disasters. How come they weren't there to begin with?

Last Thursday I was in south Florida and sat outside while the eye of Hurricane Katrina passed over my head. It was only a Category 1 then but it was pretty nasty. Eleven people died and, as of today, there were still homes without power. That night the weatherman said this storm was on its way to New Orleans. That was Thursday! Did anybody tell you? I know you didn't want to interrupt your vacation and I know how you don't like to get bad news. Plus, you had fundraisers to go to and mothers of dead soldiers to ignore and smear. You sure showed her!

I especially like how, the day after the hurricane, instead of flying to Louisiana, you flew to San Diego to party with your business peeps. Don't let people criticize you for this—after all, the hurricane was over and what the heck could you do, put your finger in the dike?

And don't listen to those who, in the coming days, will reveal how you specifically reduced the Army Corps of Engineers' budget for New Orleans this summer for the third year in a row. You just tell them that even if you hadn't cut the money to fix those levees, there weren't going to be any Army engineers to fix them anyway because you had a much more important construction job for them—BUILDING DEMOCRACY IN IRAQ!

On Day 3, when you finally left your vacation home, I have to say I was moved by how you had your Air Force One pilot descend from the clouds as you flew over New Orleans so you could catch a quick look of the disaster. Hey, I know you couldn't stop and grab a bullhorn and stand on some rubble and act like a commander in chief. Been there done that.

There will be those who will try to politicize this tragedy and try to use it against you. Just have your people keep pointing that out. Respond to nothing. Even those pesky scientists who predicted this would happen because the water in the Gulf of Mexico is getting hotter and hotter making a storm like this inevitable. Ignore them and all their global warming Chicken Littles. There is nothing unusual about a hurricane that was so wide it would be like having one F-4 tornado that stretched from New York to Cleveland.

No, Mr. Bush, you just stay the course. It's not your fault that 30 percent of New Orleans lives in poverty or that tens of thousands had no transportation to get out of town. C'mon, they're black! I mean, it's not like this happened to Kennebunkport. Can you imagine leaving white people on their roofs for five days? Don't make me laugh! Race has nothing—NOTHING—to do with this!

You hang in there, Mr. Bush. Just try to find a few of our Army helicopters and send them there. Pretend the people of New Orleans and the Gulf Coast are near Tikrit.

Yours,

Michael Moore (Moore, 2005)

An analysis of this letter must begin with the obvious method of reversal that is pervasively used in the document. Nearly every sentence is intended to mean exactly the opposite of what is stated. Most strongly, statements like "Race has nothing—NOTHING—to do with this" is a clear attack on President Bush in his handling of the aftermath of Hurricane Katrina. But again, rather than focus on whether this is an effective or entertaining example of sarcasm, it would be more germane to attend to the *function* of sarcasm in a document such as this. Moore, clearly, combines humor with a serious message here—so is it the case that the sarcasm here is used to provide a little levity to an otherwise blatant and scathing critique of President Bush?

What is Moore doing here, and why does he use sarcasm to get it done? The form of speech used here is primarily a set of commands or directives. He is directing Bush to admire himself and to do nothing to aid the unfortunate citizens of New Orleans in this crisis. The straightforward message is, "You're handling this situation really well and should be proud of your effort. Also, the situation is not a crisis because the people affected by this are not important." Of course, the real message is just the opposite. Namely, he's telling the world that Bush has botched this rescue effort and doesn't really care about these poor Black people because he's a racist.

Notice that sarcasm, generally, has a limited audience in terms of its entertainment value. In fact, its cutting nature usually divides people even more than straightforward criticism. If you agree with Moore that Bush did not act quickly nor sufficiently because he didn't really care about the victims in New Orleans, then the letter may be very entertaining. It may be so engaging that one may feel compelled to send it along to all their (similar-minded) friends and even enjoy the friends' response to the letter. "This is hilarious" might be the caption underneath the forwarded email. Those who disagree with Moore, on the other hand, would most likely be more incensed about his sarcastic letter than they would be had Moore simply laid out his argument and his contentions with how Bush had handled this situation. The sarcastic tone and form *divides* in that it maintains an "above-it-all" attitude that is haughty and condescending.

What is meant, though, by haughty? We asked the question of what value sarcasm has when compared with a straightforward critique. If Moore had simply criticized the president's handling of Hurricane Katrina by saying things like, "You should have deployed rescue resources sooner," and, even more sharply, "Your actions, or non-actions, demonstrate racism," the piece wouldn't have been nearly as entertaining. The reversals and twists that are central to sarcastic humor would be absent. But the cutting power of sarcasm would also be missing. What is missing is really an epistemic dimension of "knowing both sides" that sarcasm presents. It is akin to what we call in persuasion research a "two-sided argument" versus a "one-sided argument." By using sarcasm, the author demonstrates that he knows both sides of the situation. He is essentially saying, "I know that you want us to think that you acted effectively and want us to praise you, but that's not going to happen. You blew it!"

Soft Sarcasm

Most sarcasm, though, comes from one-liners that are either used in everyday language or presented as hypothetical "lines" that can be used to derogate a threatening person or institution.

> I find television very educating. Every time somebody turns on the set, I go into the other room and read a book.

> Experience is a wonderful thing. It enables you to recognize a mistake when you make it again. (Marx, G., 2021)

These remarks from Groucho Marx might be considered *soft sarcastic remarks* because they do not attack a particular person. In the first case, the comment focuses on the lack of educational value that television has, but it does so sarcastically by reversing the valence. Notice that the comment is a strong criticism of television; the only way to find something educational is to avoid it altogether in the form of reading a book. The second example focused on experience but represents a rare form of sarcasm that is, actually, *self-critical*. It turns on one's own inability to learn from mistakes and focuses on a general weakness of humanity.

Notice, again, how wonderfully clever and lively this utterance is when compared to the straightforward version: "We never seem to learn from mistakes but, with experience, we at least seem to recognize that we're making one when we do." By starting with, "Experience is a wonderful thing," we have a terrific setup for the unexpected twist to come. What this form of humor depends on is that the setup line is not recognized as a sarcastic one until after the completion of the second line. Now you realize that what was meant is that experience is, in fact, *not* such a wonderful thing because we never really are able to avoid making mistakes.

> Oh my God, that's so hilarious! I was in such awe of how funny it was that I forgot to laugh!

> Thank you for leaving my side when I was alone. I realized I can do so much without you! (Unknown source)

Both of these examples use the same format just described. The opening line is sarcastic—reversed in terms of the true valence intended. But it is not until the second line that one realizes the setup of the opening. Of course, these examples are much more directly cutting and directed toward the other. In the first one, the explanation of why one didn't laugh is preposterous: "I forgot to laugh." One doesn't *forget* to laugh when something is hilarious; humor is immediate, and, if something is funny, generally one cannot help but laugh. The entire utterance, then, is technically a lie. The joke wasn't hilarious, they were not in awe of how funny it was, and they certainly did not forget to laugh. Three statements are given that are all untrue, leading to a humorous, caustic proposition that what you just said was simply not funny. Of course, this would not be funny to the person who made the initial joke but only to those who enjoy the cutting humor that attacks the original joke-teller.

In the example of the person who insults their friend for leaving their side, the sarcasm begins immediately, as well, but it is not fully recognized until the second part of the statement. But the sarcasm is inherent within the first part, since one does not, generally, thank people for leaving their side in a time of need. In fact, one can argue that this example is not humorous. It's simply an insult. But it is a sarcastic, clever insult that may be considered funny by "another"—again, certainly not by the one who's being attacked.

Jonathan Swift

The most famous use of sarcasm (generally termed as "satire") still remains Jonathan Swift's essay entitled *A Modest Proposal* (1729). Swift utilizes a literary device called paraleipsis, in which he argues in favor of a quite ridiculous program of action, in which poor children would be sold to be eaten by rich families. Swift's intention is to expose the contemporary Irish aristocratic attitudes toward the poor and make a mockery of their approach to civilization. He does this by writing an essay that is very straightforward, in which he argues for the use of both cannibalism and infantilism for the greater good of Ireland.

> As to my own part, having turned my thoughts for many years, upon this important subject, and maturely weighed the several schemes of our projectors, I have always found them grossly mistaken in their computation. It is true, a child just dropt from its dam, may be supported by her milk, for a solar year, with little other nourishment: at most not above the value of two shillings, which the mother may certainly get, or the value in scraps, by her lawful occupation of begging; and it is exactly at one year old that I propose to provide for them in such a manner, as, instead of being a charge upon their parents, or the parish, or wanting food and raiment for the rest of their lives, they shall, on the contrary, contribute to the feeding, and partly to the clothing of many thousands.

There is likewise another great advantage in my scheme, that it will prevent those voluntary abortions, and that horrid practice of women murdering their bastard children, alas! too frequent among us, sacrificing the poor innocent babes, I doubt, more to avoid the expence than the shame, which would move tears and pity in the most savage and inhuman breast. (Swift, 1729, p. 1)

Our question, of course, is the value and nature of such humor. Why would Swift's intention—that we take children and the poor seriously and consider their plight—be promoted best by the use of satire of this sort? How does the tongue-in-cheek humor used here serve his purposes? For one thing, we can probably state with confidence that a straightforward essay arguing for the importance of children and for humane treatment of the poor would never have reached the notoriety that *A Modest Proposal* reached. We can certainly claim that his method worked in that sense. But what is the method, and how does it work?

By proposing the absurd, Swift leads us to the awareness of how close society is to this absurdity. By taking several steps "out there," using a currently popular phrase, Swift forces the reader to see the absurdity of modern times. We simply cannot take seriously a proposal to kill our children and feed them to the rich, however tasty they may be (he later argues for the merits of cooking children as opposed to pigs). Once the reader is in his grasp, agreeing to the absurdity of the proposal, Swift is then able to show that contemporary Irish political leaders are instituting procedures that are leading to nearly the same conclusion. We're killing our poor children by not providing opportunities for them—and this does nothing but benefit (feed) the rich.

But if we fail to notice the specific method employed, we are missing a great deal here. Sarcasm requires a direct statement (the opposite of what one is really proposing), and its success hinges on the believability of this direct statement. The essay works because of its relentlessness. Usually, a tongue-in-cheek remark is followed by its own author's laughter or nudge or wink—but Swift succeeds by continuing on, paragraph after paragraph, with more details and arguments that support his proposal. There is no "lightening" or "mediating" here; it is a truly unyielding proposal. It also does not hurt, of course, that the document is well written and cogent. It has what psychometricians call "internal consistency" in that all the arguments "hang together." This, too, creates the intensity of the march of this essay—forcing the reader to recognize its supreme absurdity and, at the same time, take it seriously in the sense of its central claim (that we need to support and nurture children and the poor).

Of course, the argument that he would personally benefit from such a practice as he is proposing is not at all one that would be used as an objection. This allows for the continuation of the absurdity of the proposition—contributing to its relentlessness and its success. The effect of this type of satire, of course, is not usually a deep belly laugh but rather a kind of painful sigh of pleasure. The reader is compelled, however, to have a friend endure the passage (or joke) at that point, and there is probably more joy in seeing the quizzical and painful reaction that the other has to it. At that point, the original reader becomes a distant "eye" who transcends the conceptual aspects of the writing and enjoys seeing the "inside" of the other's reaction. One could even argue that nobody thoroughly enjoys this type of humor, but each person continually passes it on like a chain letter to others who are forced to be exposed to it. This allows each reader to experience that moment of subjecting the other to the confusing and strange pain-pleasure combination that this form of satire provides.

Here are a few more, rather random examples of sarcasm and satire:

We must be mindful of the poor and unfortunate. It is the easiest way to feel better about our own lot in life.

The best things in life are free—until someone figures out how to make money from them.

I have had a perfectly wonderful evening—but this wasn't it.

Some cause happiness wherever they go, others whenever they go.

I didn't attend the funeral—but I sent a nice letter saying that I approved of it.

He is a self-made man—and worships his creator.

Those who believe in telekinetics, please raise my hand. (Sources Unknown)

Are there definitive patterns in these types of sarcastic utterances? One very obvious one is the movement from positive to negative valence. The first part of each statement is an innocent, positive declaration, but the second part is a cynical negation of the first. Again, the pleasure is mostly in catching the other unawares—first, trapping them in the innocence of the original statement and then lowering the boom on them with the undoing of that innocence. Life is not all good; when it appears so, you're probably just in a kind of illusion. In the current list, we find cynicism about: 1) sympathy for the poor, 2) egotism, 3) human nature, and 4) magical beliefs. Most sarcasm, though, centers on human nature and greed, with the upshot being that we are essentially self-serving, narcissistic, and Machiavellian—even when there is an appearance of innocence.

There are rather extensive lists of sarcastic quips or one-liners that would qualify as sarcastic in nature. In fact, organizations such as the Sarcastic Society have emerged with websites filled with quips, quotes, and news articles that provide sarcastic twists and turns designed to entertain. But one can fairly easily notice that this is more than entertainment. There are consistent themes that lie underneath the "sarcastic approach" to life, and there are people who "live for sarcasm" in that it provides their primary relation to others and to life in general. What is this approach to life, though—and how does it function for the person who embraces it?

Lenny Bruce and Political Satire

Lenny Bruce's comic act was truly revolutionary. His performances and writings defy strict categorization, in terms of our classic forms of humor. He used a great deal of sarcasm to expose both political and social hypocrisies in American culture. Although this category of satire-sarcasm does not capture anywhere near the full range of Bruce's work, his use of sarcasm and satire was, perhaps, his most lethal weapon in combating unethical and irrational governmental laws and policies.

> But dangerous drugs, the connection is Park-Lilly. It's Olin Mathieson. The only difference between a "felon drug user" and the everyday man is that the felon can't afford a prescription—so they legislate against poor people.

> Do you know how much I love the Post Office? I love the Post Man so much. I really feel that's the only place where the authority and the man are one. That's the man, they're incorruptible. . . . Like that, Post Office, going through snow and sleet. But they don't like when dogs bite them. That's one thing, they won't put up with any shit. The dog bites? That's it, we're not delivering any more mail to you. (Bruce, 1965)

Bruce challenged many of our institutions, customs, and attitudes in a powerful, satirical, humorous way—which landed him in jail repeatedly for obscenity (as well as narcotics charges). One of his primary areas of attack was our puritanical view of sexuality.

We Americans have a negative attitude towards prostitution that is not shared by foreign peoples. Even the words, "French Brothel" sound exotic, nearly romantic, compared to "Cathouse." And they are more romantic. They cater to the imagination and the spirit as well as the body. Here, it's disgustingly cut and dry. (Bruce, 1965, p. 41)

When it came to politicians, Bruce was very aware of his own limitations in knowing which ones were better than others.

I voted in the 1960 Presidential election, but I didn't get too emotionally involved and vehement with the attitude that, "My man is the best man," because I didn't know the man I voted for. I think the cliché is that you don't know a man till you live with him, and since I never slept with Nixon or Kennedy, I can only tell you if they were good in retrospect. (Bruce, 1965, p. 185)

That amazing mix of humor, skepticism, sarcasm, and humility will probably never be reproduced again. Unfortunately, Bruce suffered from relationship problems, financial difficulties, legal issues, and drug abuse and ultimately died of a drug overdose at the age of 40. He served as a pioneer for political, sexual, and satirical humor. I think we can safely say that there will never be another Lenny Bruce.

The Daily Show

If you're tired of the stodginess of the evening newscasts, if you can't bear to sit through the spinmeisters and shills on the 24-hour cable news networks, don't miss *The Daily Show with Jon Stewart*, a nightly half-hour series unburdened by objectivity, journalistic integrity, or even accuracy. (IGN, 2015)

If you're thinking that sarcasm is relegated to minor quips and jokes that are uttered sporadically in our society, think again. *The Daily Show* and *The Colbert Report* (now called *The Late Show*) and, to some extent, *Late Night with Seth Meyers* have brought sarcasm and satire to the forefront in American culture. They are so popular—especially among young people, that more people are getting their "news" from these shows than from the traditional news shows today. Many people describe their experience of taking in these satirical shows as "a relief" from the drudgery of their daily life.

At first glance, we could easily minimize the importance of *The Daily Show*, Colbert's shows, and Seth Meyers's *Late Night* shows as simply entertainment. They provide a satirical look at the political and news realms and poke fun at the major players in those arenas. Why would people gravitate to such a forum? All manner of explanations has been offered—including the need to escape (given bad economic times), the charismatic nature of the personalities anchoring these shows, and the increased hypocrisy and corruption in government. Some years ago, the general conclusion was that young people were not interested in politics; now, with the success of these shows, we have been forced to recognize that young people are, in fact, interested in politics and news—just not as it was, generally, presented by the networks.

Even more interesting, though, is the connection between sarcasm, satire, and truth. Viewers of these politically based comedic shows argue that they watch for entertainment but also because they are given the most direct, frank, truthful presentation of the news here. In one way, it appears that the sarcastic, comedic approach adopted actually allows for a more honest approach to the news story. Jon Stewart, Trevor Noah, and Stephen Colbert utilized the comedic format to facilitate powerful, critical views of hypocrisy, corruption, and scandalous political behavior.

At first the difference will be in whatever atmosphere I bring into it. It's not going to be like, "I really want to do *The Daily Show* and I'd love to turn it into an abstract musical." I like the format and the chance to satirize the news.

The Internet is just a world passing around notes in a classroom.

Religion. It's given people hope in a world torn apart by religion.

When a political party stands together, there is nothing it can't prevent from getting done.

(Stewart, in AZ Quotes, 2021)

What Stewart, Noah, and Colbert provide their audience is allowing them to enjoy the guilty pleasure of sarcasm while they, themselves, are passive observers. The comic "sacrifices himself" in the moment of delivery. The audience member is allowed to be engaged without the burden (guilt) of being the *source* of the sarcasm. "Oh," she says, "I would never go that far," as Colbert takes that extra step in making fun of the president or Congress or whatever authority he picks on. This affords us the opportunity to not be responsible for such a "cheap shot," but we are, generally, pleased that the comic does this for us.

Of course, one of the easiest of targets is the corporate world. Again, though, Stewart, Noah, and Colbert are willing to just go that "extra yard" beyond what we would be comfortable expressing. Another striking aspect is the uniquely American nature of political satire. Whereas other countries clearly have political humor, the degree of satire and the daily (excuse the pun) dose that we are exposed to from the late-night comics is extraordinary. It's as if we cannot survive even a day without being able to "undo" the awfulness of American political life with a quip or a stab from the comedians. The late-night satire allows us to clean the slate and be able to lie down and rest—otherwise the sheer torture of American political life would leave us sleepless.

What, though, is the sarcastic person doing as he or she is engaged in sarcasm itself? We have explored satire from the standpoint of the receiver but what about that person who cannot live without the *use* of satire in their daily life?

The Sarcastic Personality

We can all probably name a person or two who uses sarcasm and satire as an integral part of their social relations. They might be described as cynical or perhaps as one who is "always making fun of things" or one who "cannot take anything seriously." In fact, others often remark about such a person that "you can never tell when they're serious" because they use sarcastic humor so consistently. Of course, the type of sarcasm that is consistently used plays a major role in the psychology of the person using it. Martin and Ford (2018) correctly point out that humor can be either other-directed or self-directed—and this is very true of sarcasm. The person who directs their sarcasm at ridiculing the other is quite different from one who uses self-deprecating sarcasm for social purposes, which we will consider in chapter six.

> He's a great teacher. Yeah, he's great if you need to catch up on sleep. Have you ever managed to stay awake through one of his lectures? If so, you deserve an award.

> What am I up to these days? Actually, I'm applying to law schools. As if a good law school would be stupid enough to accept me! (fictional examples)

Obviously, the other-directed sarcastic person has issues with anger, bitterness, and probably resentment. They use sarcasm to defeat the other as a threat—by showing how preposterous the claims of the other are. The most common critiques that the sarcastic person engages in are that the world (but, usually, in a particular example) is not lively and entertaining and/or that people are not considerate or intelligent. They lodge a complaint through their sarcasm, and, if the listener responds with sympathetic laughter, they have gained a kind of victory over the other and the external world in general.

What, though, distinguishes the sarcastic person from a simply angry, bitter, hostile person who expresses themselves more directly? Herein lies the power of sarcasm—its indirectness. The satirist is able to present a critique without actually asserting a statement. They do not have to "take on" the other with whom they are contentious but rather fire out a quip that combines humor and critique at the same time. They can hide behind the humor without having to stand behind the critique. If the other laughs, they have agreed with the critique and also acknowledged the cleverness of the satirist, while the arguments that the satirist provides are not fully recognized or revealed. When it works best, sarcasm provides a *quick strike* that reduces or even destroys the enemy without having to engage in direct combat.

How, though, does the humor work here? The moment of humor seems to serve to break the conflict of opinion and allow for the introduction of a positive feeling. Although the critique may be deadly, the laughter it provides is playful and positive, strangely enough. Swift has us laughing, which breaks the spirit of conflict and, instead, leaves us enjoying the cleverness of his points. The satirist, then, can win the favor of the other by instilling a positive, laughing experience even while they are, essentially, a critic.

Thus far, however, we're assuming success on the part of the satirist—with their quick strikes and clever reductions. But, in fact, sarcasm is one of the riskier propositions when it comes to humor. Many things can go wrong in the process of satire or sarcasm. Some people simply do not like this form of humor and are not humored by it whatsoever. Some do not "get" the sarcastic position and mis-interpret the point completely. When the other truly feels strongly about their political or social position (when it's contrary to that of the satirist), moreover, they are not very likely to be amused by the satirist. On the contrary, they are likely to be annoyed or irritated with such a person.

Even more damning, however, is the fact that few people can tolerate a steady diet of sarcasm. They may be temporarily amused and even admiring of the satirist but, after more substantial engage-ment, are often tired of such cynicism. Usually, the satirist finds one person to whom they can express their views and make their quips—a "straight person" of sorts who, because of their own per-sonality (and perhaps deficits), is impressed and engaged by this type of person. But seldom is the satirist truly a continued hit at parties and social gatherings. In general, satire and sarcasm are not a winning strategy in the social world.

> At an informal lunch amongst professors, one of the professors utters, "I really think our university president is in complete con-trol of things. He has a master plan." (fictional vignette)

The sarcastic remarks are made for the *benefit* of the other pro-fessors. Sarcasm is inherently social. Without an audience, it loses its meaning and power. Can you imagine someone writing sarcasti-cally in a journal that was not intended to ever be read by another? One clue to this is the notion of biting sarcastic humor. One cannot bite without "biting down" on something; sarcasm is meant to *have an effect* on the other. Even when one is writing sarcastically, there is the implied audience who will receive this "bite" and the imagined effect it will have. What is that effect, though?

The dominant *intent* for the satiric personality is the destruction of naivety. The cynical professor, in the example given, is disturbed by the naivety of others. Their naivety is actually a threat to them, which he must overcome. Arguing about the competence of the university president is less effective than using the biting sarcasm of a quip that both distances him (in an almost condescending manner) and demonstrates his superiority to both the president and the others. If they "buy in" to the sarcasm, they no longer stand in opposition to the cynic and are connected to him through the medium of sarcastic humor. They no longer serve as naive obstacles but as enlightened compatriots. The risk, however, is that they will turn on the cynic and see them as an ego for maintaining both distance and anger. Sarcasm is a manipulation of the social world—one that can have dramatically positive but also possibly quite negative effects.

In fact, there is an ironic quality to the whole dance to which we refer. Naivete must continue to exist in order for the satirist to have their day. Innocence is what they feed on and depend on—yet it is also precisely what they need to overcome and destroy. They are continually annoyed at the presence and degree of naivety—"Can you believe she actually believes that this is an effective university president?"—yet they cannot use their weapon without the existence of that naivety. This is, perhaps, why the satirist typically connects interpersonally with people who do not share their cynical view of life. The naive person and the satirist thrive on each other, each providing a missing element that they need but don't wish to possess within themselves as personal traits. "I just wouldn't know how to live life if I was as cynical and negative as you are," remarks the innocent—while the satirist argues, "I can't imagine how you can go through life with such simple and naive beliefs."

Chapter 5

LANGUAGE HUMOR

This subject matter certainly warrants an entire work devoted to it. For now, though, we can look at language humor as a curious blend of highbrow humor and pure silliness. One of my favorite examples comes from comedian Brian Regan (2012):

> I was thinking about visiting a Native American community. In fact, I made a plan to visit. But then I had second thoughts about the visit. So—I guess you could say I had a "reservation reservation reservation."

One can recognize language humor by the fact that, clearly, there is nothing humorous about this tale except for the final articulation of language. Considering a visit, then making a plan, then having reservations about that visit is simply not funny. In fact, it's decidedly mundane. The humor in this quip lies entirely in the oddity of being able to (correctly, actually) use the same word consecutively three times. Of course, repetition is often a path to humor. A child uttering, "Daddy, daddy, daddy, daddy" can be funny in itself. But "reservation reservation reservation" is extremely clever because it demonstrates that language can do funny things that allow for an utterance to sound completely absurd while retaining correct grammar and syntax.

Each of the "reservations" represents a different use of the word. The first "reservation" refers to the noun that represents a place that Native Americans may live. The second one is a plan or agreement to visit; we make reservations as a commitment to visit. The third is a set of mental "events," as we may have doubts concerning the value of such a visit. Of course, if you "got it" right away, this detailed explanation probably just diminished the power of the joke!

> Yesterday I accidentally swallowed some food coloring. The doctor says I'm OK, but I feel like I've dyed a little inside.
>
> Have you ever tried to eat a clock? It's very time-consuming.
>
> I wasn't originally going to get a brain transplant, but then I changed my mind.
>
> "Doctor! Doctor! Help! I think I'm shrinking!" "Calm down, please. You'll just have to be a little patient."
>
> Two peanuts were walking in the park. One was a salted. (Post Randomonium, 2021)

Language humor characteristically utilizes double meanings of various sorts. The first one in this sequence turns on the simple word "died" being the same pronunciation as "dyed." Another necessary ingredient may be the dramatic twist, as each of these examples seem to display. There must be something of some importance that captures the listener. Otherwise, there is nothing to pay attention to or care about—nothing that is in jeopardy. In each case, a statement is made in a rather commanding fashion. This "seriousness" is part of the equation that is later contrasted with the silliness of the joke. The double meaning, then, allows the statement to mean something entirely different. The new meaning sends the receiver of the language joke into a recognition of the "silly." What is that recognition, though?

Part of it is simply the contrast between two seemingly different meanings. What is *revealed* in this form of humor is just how precarious language is—how close we come to extreme, unintended meanings. Sometimes this humor appears as a function of "autocorrect" programs that lead to miscommunication. It is as if this form of humor is revelatory about the danger of language in that it relies on very slight distinctions in sound and meaning. The arbitrary nature of language content and rules is explored and played with in language humor.

Lou Costello: Well, then, who's on first?

Bud Abbott: Yes.

Lou Costello: I mean the fellow's name.

Bud Abbott: Who.

Lou Costello: The guy on first.

Bud Abbott: Who.

Lou Costello: The first baseman.

Bud Abbott: Who.

Lou Costello: The guy playing . . .

Bud Abbott: Who is on first!

Lou Costello: I'm asking YOU who's on first.

Bud Abbott: That's the man's name.

Lou Costello: That's who's name? (Abbott & Costello, 1940/2021)

The famous "Who's on First" routine, which is now proudly displayed in the Baseball Hall of Fame, is a brilliant, clever, masterfully presented demonstration of language humor. It is based on the simple premise that a word with a certain meaning can also serve as a proper name, providing a tremendous opportunity for misunderstanding. "Who's" on first, "What's" on second, and "I-don't-know's" on third—all represent language that is not generally used for names, but since there are no "real rules" for names, here come the misunderstandings! There is nothing that stops us from naming a person "Who" or "What" or even "I don't know"—but this leads to a very delicious serving of confusion, brilliantly performed by the duo.

Is it a good thing if a vacuum really sucks?

A Freudian slip is when you say one thing but mean your mother.

I can't believe I got fired from the calendar factory. All I did was take a day off. (Punpedia, 2021)

The word "sucks" is used in two very different contexts—one simply meaning "poor" or "unsatisfying," as in "this food sucks." Of course, the more literal meaning of the word refers to a sharp action of intake. In ordinary contexts, we can even see a parallel between the colloquial use of the word as in "that movie sucked" where the content of the movie "sucked" your attention unjustifiably or "sucked some money" out of your pocketbook. But in the case of a vacuum, sucking is what is desired. Contrasting both meanings produces the humor.

In the case of the Freudian slip, the word "mother" is substituted for "another," which allows for the surprise ending in this quip. What is even more clever is that "mother" is a prominent content area for the Freudian approach, thus allowing the statement to reflexively validate itself. Quite brilliant! Perhaps the funniest aspect of the "calendar factory" is just that—how often do we think of calendars as having a factory? Thus, the reader is tipped off that something is awry or odd, and then the punchline is delivered by utilizing the concept of "taking a day off," which is a common phrase that, here, packs the double meaning.

When I get naked in the bathroom, the shower usually gets turned on.

Why did the scientist install a knocker on his door? He wanted to win the no-bell prize!

Thieves had broken into my house and stolen everything except my soap, shower gel, towels, and deodorant. Dirty Bastards! (Hahahumor, 2021)

Patterns in Language Humor

Is there a recognizable pattern in language humor? The word "clever" might be most appropriate. The *creator* of the language humor has thought beyond the ordinary usage of language and utilized the arbitrariness of syntax and semantics to extend the language into absurdity. The receiver, on the other hand, gets a chance to be first surprised and then to penetrate the double meaning such that the joke is perceived.

Having sex in an elevator is wrong on so many levels.

My math teacher called me average. How mean! (Comicbook and beyond, 2019)

The first of these examples runs the risk of "not being caught" by the general public because of the prevalence of phrases such as "wrong on so many levels" in our daily talk. Also, the moralism of the message is quite common. The joke can easily be lost. This is, of course, a danger of language humor because the punchline is the "whole thing" in this type of humor. The math joke is one that is accessible to those who study the mean, the mode, and the median—but not likely so for the average person (excuse the pun).

How can you spot the blind guy at the nudist colony? It's not hard.

A hole was found in the wall of a nudist camp. The police are looking into it.

Nudist Resort Sign: "Sorry—Clothed for Winter" (Upjoke, 2021)

These nudist colony jokes prey on the lower element in our nature and its contrast with the expressed goals of nudist colonies. They would claim to be aiming at a kind of natural life, free of constraints, rules, and hang-ups. But nearly every joke about nudist colonies has, at its root, the obvious sexual aspect of nudity as its centerpiece. The interest in looking at nudes in a sexual manner, dismissed by the articulated or expressed goal, returns in the form of humor that highlights that factor and contrasts it with the innocent and naive goals of such an endeavor. Language, then, is just one subtle manner of revealing that contrast.

In democracy, it's your vote that counts. In feudalism, it's your count that votes.

Santa's elves are just a bunch of Clauses.

"Does this restaurant serve crabs?" "Sure. Come on in, we serve everyone!" (Reddit, 2021)

These one-liners or short language jokes are fairly well stripped down to bare language manipulation. Much of this sort of humor hinges on the *reversibility* of language—that one word—for example, crabs—can refer to more than one meaning. Santa Claus and the word "clause" have completely different meanings while sharing the same sounds. One can marvel at the way that the same manifestation is used for two distinct meanings. These one-liners utilize this to contrast and compare those two iterations.

A restaurant had a sign that said, "Breakfast anytime." So I went in and ordered French Toast during the Renaissance.

What if there were no hypothetical questions?

Hyphenated. Non-hyphenated. The irony. (Wright, 2016)

The simple word "anytime" can clearly mean "anytime during the day" or "anytime in history," and Steven Wright is playing with that ambiguity here. The second and third of these one-liners reveal a very deep philosophical question, actually. It is the classic problem of reflexivity that Russell and Whitehead (1925) worked on at the turn of the 20th century. The question cannot be answered in a consistent manner. If there are, as the question implies, no hypothetical questions, then there is a contradiction since the question itself is hypothetical in nature so there both are and aren't hypotheticals. But if there are no hypotheticals, then the question is a true hypothetical and therefore, we are in a contradiction once again.

In the case of the hyphenated versus non-hyphenated example, the problem lies in the dual expression involved in language. One is the syntactical, written articulation of thought, whereas the other is semantic meaning. When we cross those two, we can arrive at absurd or apparent contradictions or at least ironic formulations. Such is the case, too, with many of the grammar jokes.

The past, the present, and the future walked into a bar. It was tense.

I will always be disappointed that a group of squids is not called a squad.

My English teacher looked my way and said, "Name two pronouns." I said, "Who, me?"

When two English majors marry: "I now pronouns you he and she."

We need hyphens! Because working twenty four-hour shifts is not the same as working twenty-four hour shifts or twenty-four-hour shifts.

First rule of the Thesaurus Club: don't talk, discuss, converse, speak, chat, confer, deliberate, gab, or gossip about the Thesaurus Club. (Reddit, 2021)

To some extent, these jokes are enjoyed only by those who take grammar seriously. The appreciation of such humor is not widespread and probably represents a niche humor domain. They are sent around the internet, posted on professors' doors, and used as examples in college classrooms. This humor does not make it to *Saturday Night Live* or even comics' performances. But it contains some powerful elements of the essence of humor, nonetheless.

The joke about working shifts is both instructive from the standpoint of the consequences of poor grammar and also humorous—and for the same reason. One little hyphen, thought to be a slight accent on the meaning of an expression, can have such a dramatic effect on the stated truth. Besides the obvious "grammar lesson" inherent, though, wherein lies the humor? Again, this type of humor is not the belly-laugh humor of, say, physical humor, but rather the chuckle-based transcendence of the sophisticated learner. Through this "brainteaser," we come to know that a mere hyphen can dramatically change meaning, for it is one thing to work 20 four-hour shifts, another to work 24-hour shifts—and still another to simply work one-hour shifts 24 times!

One of my favorite jokes was used by the best man at a wedding I attended. One of my oldest friends, John, who was never a therapy patient, himself, was marrying a woman who was a psychiatrist. His brother began his "best man" speech by saying, "When John announced to the family that he was *seeing* a psychiatrist, I said, 'Hallelujah!' Finally he's getting some help! But then he told us that he was 'seeing' a psychiatrist." (permission granted by those involved but anonymity requested)

John's brother was playing with the different meanings of the word "seeing," which obviously can mean both being a psychother-apy client as well as romantic dating. But, of course, he was also engaging in some good-natured ribbing of his brother, the groom. Thirty-seven years later, John is still "seeing" that same psychiatrist.

Idioms and Language Humor

I'm fit to be tied. You're driving me up the wall. Don't let the cat out of the bag!

Break a leg! He's got a chip on his shoulder. If this doesn't work, it's back to the drawing board. That was the straw that broke the camel's back. (Dais, 2021)

English idioms provide quite a challenge to the non-native speaker—and there are so many of them (possibly as many as 25,000). But they also can be the source of much humor when the innocent mind approaches an idiom in a concrete, literal fashion. "What cat is in what bag? I don't see a chip on his shoulder, Mom. Do we have a camel somewhere that I haven't seen?" In fact, a book called *Unintentional Humor: Celebrating the Literal Mind* (Ander-son, 2011) was written by the mother of an autistic child, which features the drawings of the child as he attempts to come to grips with these common English-language idioms.

Another form of language humor that capitalizes on this "alien" or "other" perspective occurs when an alien species encounters the ordinary life of the native speakers. One such fictional encounter was created in the very popular sitcom of *Mork & Mindy* (Marshall

& Marshall, 1978–1982). Robin Williams brilliantly portrayed the character, Mork, who came from another solar system, from a planet named Ork, and encountered Mindy, an ordinary but also adorable young woman.

The audience was entertained by the freshness and naivety of Mork as he encountered modern American life and, just as important, the idiosyncrasies of our language. The show used the "Orkan" greeting—Na-Nu Na-Nu—to remind us that Mork was, indeed, "other." He consistently made innocent mistakes because of his lack of knowledge of English idioms or mores. The show was considered a huge success, though it struggled after four years and was, finally, pulled after the completion of the fourth season.

Misrepresentations, Excessiveness, and Euphemisms

George Carlin investigated many of our English-language expressions for misrepresentation, excessiveness, and euphemisms. He pointed out the absurdity involved in many commonly used phrases and statements.

> "The country is going down the tubes," people say. What tubes are we talking about? And why are there more than one? Seems to me that it might make sense for there to just be one tube for each country, no?

> "He was legally drunk at the time of the incident." If he were "legally" drunk, then what is the problem?

> "I'd be more than happy to do that for you." How can you be more than happy? This sounds like a dangerous mental condition.

> "Tell us 'in your own words' what happened that day." Does anyone have their own words? Don't we all pretty much use the same words that everyone else is using? (Carlin, 1988)

Carlin (1988) also tells us that we love *soft language*—euphemisms—as opposed to telling the truth. And this problem keeps getting worse with each generation.

> In the first World War, we used the term "shell-shocked" for a soldier whose nervous system was overwhelmed by combat. By World War II, we lengthened it to "Combat Fatigue." Fatigue is a nice word, softer than shocked. In the Korean War, we changed the very-same condition to be called "Operational Exhaustion." This sounds like something that could occur to your car, no? And in the Vietnam War, we began using the term "Post Traumatic Stress Disorder." Now the pain is completely buried under jargon.

In *The Denial of Death* (1973), Ernest Becker proposed that both our societal practices and our individual motivation are centered on diminishing or even dismissing the looming prospect of death. Much of our language around death is, in Carlin's perspective, "soft." He "passed away," she "is no longer with us," she "went peacefully," etc. As Carlin says, the pain is buried under jargon. Language is used to cover up the grim realities of life and death. At its most extreme, this can result in humor, as the contrast is highlighted between the niceties of the common description with the stripped-down truth. Carlin (1988) continues:

> Sometime during my lifetime, "toilet paper" became "bathroom tissue." "Sneakers" became "running shoes." "False teeth" became "dental appliances." "The dump" became "the landfill." "Car crashes" became "automobile accidents." "House trailers" became "mobile homes." "Constipation" became "occasional irregularity." Deaf became "hearing impaired." Blind is now "visually impaired."

Another theme Carlin (2001) explores is the modern tendency to use language to accentuate, exaggerate, or aggrandize.

People add words when they want things to sound more important than they really are. "Boarding process." Sounds important. It isn't. It's just a bunch of people getting on an airplane! People like to sound important. Weathermen on television talk about "shower activity." Sounds more important than "showers." I even heard one guy on CNN talk about a "rain event." I swear to God, he said, "Louisiana is expecting a rain event." And I thought, "Holy shit, I hope I can get tickets to that!"

Many words, in fact, have been lengthened rather than simplified in recent times. My students use the word "empathetic" rather than the simpler "empathic." Sports announcers refer to a "dominating" performance rather than a "dominant" performance. Names have become more complex. What happened to Bob, Jim, Joe, Jill, Sue, and Deb? Our interest in the longer, more impressive, and more complex is, in fact, the fodder for humor in that language attempts to mask the simple, basic truths. It's raining; this is not a "rain event." It's a storm, not "storm activity."

Of course, the whole concept of language humor is a bit of a misnomer since nearly all humor (aside from physical humor) involves language to a large extent. I often marvel at the way in which language needs to be used in an incredibly precise and exact manner in humor. For example, one of my favorite childhood (and adult, I must admit) jokes is the following:

Customer: Waiter, waiter—what's that fly doing in my soup?

Waiter: I believe that is "the backstroke." (Unknown source)

As a little thought experiment, try to rewrite this joke by changing the customer's question—just slightly. It is, largely, impossible. "Why is there a fly in my soup?" "Can you explain why there is a fly in my soup?" The emphasis must be on the "doing" aspect while retaining the indignation of finding a bug in one's soup. The language, then, must be very precise—to say nothing of the tone, timing, and other aspects of joke-telling that are ingredients in its success.

Those Who Value and Use Language Humor

Language humor tends to divide the crowd. Those who employ it seem to continually delight in every new pun, language twist, double entendre, and innocent mistake that they can find. Others find no particular value in the exercise and, in fact, may complain that the language joke is foolish, not particularly clever, or, more likely, simply not terribly funny. What makes the lover of this form of humor so enamored with it, then?

The delighter seems to revel in the *flexibility* of language. One slight change can produce an enormous shift of meaning. One slip produces a completely opposite implication. A slightly different interpretation, due to the indefinite nature of language, produces a wildly variant result. Much of this is a delight in the contrast effect; one attempts to compliment a person but, mistakenly, winds up insulting them. One is attempting to be polite but transverses the mores of the culture and the opposite result ensues. The same word can be used with completely different meanings.

But the "punner" also seems to need a "straight person," an innocent, naive person who does not, at least immediately, "get it" or embrace the nuance that the delighter already recognizes. In the straight person's recognition comes the moment of transcendence for the appreciator of language humor. They are, then, able, through pointing out to the other, to stand outside the ordinary use of language and become a kind of omniscient observer.

In fact, there is probably more enjoyment for the teller of language humor jokes than for the receiver. The receiver is taken by surprise and more likely to only appreciate the pun or twist of language *later* or as they are able to relay the joke to another. As with most humor, the social aspect is critical—but, in this case, it is almost as if the receiver is a kind of victim of innocence while the teller wields all the power. Of course, the teller of the language joke must attempt to find a suitable target—one who will, in the end, grant the cleverness of the utterance—but this may not even be critical to the teller since they are completely absorbed in the excitement of the language twist. If the other wishes to share that delectable and enjoy it as well, that is fine, but the pastry tastes great on its own and in and of itself.

Chapter 6

SELF-DEPRECATING HUMOR

I don't want to belong to any club that would accept me as one of its members. (Marx, 1949)

M any versions of this quote have been used over the years by various comedians—most notably, Woody Allen. Legend has it that Groucho Marx stated this as his reason for resigning from the Friars Club in Hollywood in the late 1940s. Hollywood columnist Erskine Johnson popularized the tale in the *St. Petersburg Times* in November 1949.

Self-deprecating humor appears to have emerged as a form of humor only in the last century. In fact, given our modern perspective, it is particularly striking that wise men such as Plato, as discussed by Morreall (2009), did not anticipate anything like self-deprecating humor. His criticism of comedy in general, in fact, seems to not admit of this form of humor and only addresses the kind of *externalizing humor* where we laugh at the plight of others. But if self-deprecating humor can be considered a viable candidate in itself, it would serve to soften or even make irrelevant the Platonic view of humor as selfish, base, and indulgent.

In fact, self-deprecating humor might have its own historical narrative that is, indeed, separate from the history of humor in general. One can trace self-deprecation from the physical comedy of Buster Keaton to the Little Tramp of Chaplin to the Marx Brothers to Woody Allen—and a host of other modern comics who have employed self-deprecating humor in their craft. Why would this form of humor be so dormant as to never even be referred to or mentioned prior to the 20th century?

> I'm not very good at dating. This is how I used to hit on guys. I used to stand next to them . . . for years. (Kashian, in AZ Quotes, 2019)

> I spent seven hours in a beauty shop . . . and that was for the estimate. (Diller, in AZ Quotes, 2021)

What, then, is the nature of humor that pokes fun at oneself? What could be the value or function of such humor? One obvious factor to consider in self-deprecating humor is the social value that this form of humor may provide. If I make fun of myself, this facilitates a social bond with the other, who finds this humor funny. It is the ultimate icebreaker, which evolutionists would see as akin to laying one's weapons down and making it clear that one is no threat to the other. If I am admitting my own weakness in the moment of self-deprecation, then this is, in effect, allowing the other to be empowered and drawing them into a stronger social connection. Self-deprecating humor as a social strategy of disarming oneself in relation to the other, then, is perfectly understandable and functions as a way of engaging with and connecting with others.

> I'm short enough and ugly enough to succeed on my own.

> How am I immature? Intellectually, emotionally, and sexually. Yeah, but in what other ways?

> Most of the time I don't have much fun; the rest of the time I don't have any fun at all.

> I'm one of the few *men* who suffer from penis envy. (Allen, 2021)

But is that all there is to self-deprecating humor? What about the audience who is watching Woody Allen on screen? They are clearly not going to interact with him in person but, nevertheless, may enjoy his antics as they watch. If self-deprecating humor was simply about social engagement, then why would it work on screen in comedic films? What is the relation that the audience has to the actors or comedians as they watch Groucho Marx, Charlie Chaplin, or Woody Allen make fun of themselves?

> I got my first bikini. It's a three-piece—a top, a bottom, and a blindfold for you to wear.

> I go running when I have to . . . when the ice cream truck is doing 60! (Liebman, 2021)

There is also the question of what the humor is in self-deprecating humor. If this is simply a form of disarming oneself to smooth the waters of social interaction, what is the humor component? One could disarm oneself, after all, without the element of humor by pointing out one's weaknesses and faults—a strategy that social psychologists call *self-handicapping* (Kolditz & Arkin, 1982). But here we are concerned with a form of humor—and one that is quite commonly utilized, especially by comedians.

It would be easy to claim that the audience member gets a kind of sinister glee at seeing the self-deprecating fool admit to and poke fun at his own weaknesses. But there is more to the story. In fact, this form of humor allows for the audience member to *relate to* the character; indeed, it *depends on* the audience member relating. This is why many people cannot engage with self-deprecating humor; they cannot allow themselves to be seen or to see themselves in that light.

There seem to be two different ways to deal with life's negative aspects: deny them or embrace them. Some deny it (what some psychologists called the "deniers") and push against the negative aspects with all their might, insisting there is "nothing wrong" in life. Others embrace it (what some psychologists called the "embracers"). That's the tact self-deprecating comics take; they recognize the inevitability of conflict, negative outcomes, and fatality. They then universalize it in the sense that the comic gesture, if successful, demonstrates that "this can happen to anyone." In the final stage, however, they distance themselves from being the lonely subject of that negative situation—and ask the audience member to participate in that universalization and transcendent laughing. At the moment of humor, then, the self-deprecating comic is free of creaturehood and transcendent to the tragic life being made fun of.

If, on the other hand, the self-deprecating comic is simply viewed as a loser, then the project, of course, fails. This form of humor depends upon the audience member *relating with* the comedian, who is succumbing to the difficulties that appear to be *inherent* in life. Self-deprecating humor, then, is a risky maneuver that can end with failure when the other refuses to enter into the tragic vision of the comedian. In fact, many people do not "get" Woody Allen's form of humor and just see him as a pathetic loser who is somehow indulging in his own foolishness in a desperate attempt to engage his audience. Of course, his personal life and much publicized accusations against him did not help his public persona much at all.

> I was told at the doctor's office that I should get a facelift. The doctor agreed with the waiting room when he came out.
>
> I'm in shape. Round is a shape, right?
>
> Someone asked if I knew a good plastic surgeon. Would I look like this if I did? (Allen, 2021)

Promotion of the Self Leads to Self-Deprecating Humor

These appearance-oriented self-deprecations allow the other to immediately enter into laughing at the comedian. What are we laughing at? One key ingredient is the relief we feel from the self-propagation that serves as a kind of norm in interpersonal relations. This self-propagation entails putting your "best foot forward." Baumeister and his colleagues (2007) have argued, convincingly, that the *promotion of the self* has been the single most powerful development, psychologically, in the past century. The self-esteem movement in which everyone is encouraged to see themselves as "special" is part of this. Think of the emphasis placed on "everyone being a winner" that is exemplified in giving all children trophies and awards for simply performing minimally impressive tasks.

The contrast between self-promotion and self-deprecation satisfies one of the most important dimensions of humor: surprise. In the self-deprecation moment, moreover, we are *relieved* from that project to promote the self. Even more appealing for the viewer of self-deprecating humor is the fact that the deprecation is in the other, not in the receiver, of that humor. Let's return to the central one-liner with which this chapter began, that I wouldn't want to be a member of a club that would have me as a member. This classic, self-deprecating statement illustrates much of the essence of the self-deprecating gesture.

The statement, though, can be broken into two essential aspects. The first and most direct interpretation of the statement is that the organization's standards must be very low in order to accept a person that is so worthless as I am. It's a self-demeaning statement that derogates one's own standing.

The second part—and the part that is perhaps most humorous—is that the person, themselves, has standards that are too high to accept one's own membership in a club they seek membership in. This implies a twofold sense of self in which one is the bodily, basic entity (which is quite lousy and unacceptable) and the other, a critical dimension that rejects the organization precisely because its standards are too low to reject a person who is so worthless. The self-deprecator, then, has the *awareness* of their limitations such that they evaluate themselves and know themselves to be what they are—quite unworthy.

It is this awareness, though, of their own value and the critical dimension, applied to the organization, that both makes the joke funny and also reveals the duality in self-deprecation. The comic, in this case, is both "in it" as the lowly "body" and is also transcendent as the knower of that body and critic of the other (organization). But simply knowing one's status and that organizations have standards, and seeking membership in that organization, would not be humorous. It would, in fact, be more on the sad or even on the pathetic side. But it is the act of rejecting the organization for its lax standards that provides the comedy because now the incongruity between recognizing yourself as lowly and maintaining high standards—even higher than the organization you're a candidate for membership in—becomes evident, providing the humor and also the transcendence.

Self-Deprecating Humor for the Comic

> I like to think when I play a club, while I don't always entertain the audience, they certainly feel better leaving because they're not me. (Shandling, in Kronke, 1995)

On the surface, it would seem as if self-deprecating humor would provide almost nothing for the performer of that humor. Of course, it would serve as an icebreaker on the social level and allow for a connection with some of his or her audience—but this does not seem enough to warrant or justify making a fool of oneself, which is required in this form of humor. The hidden mystery is how the self-deprecator benefits from being the source of this humor. It is as if they transcend the situation by hovering above as superior to the person who is making a fool of himself. It is a rather striking reality that nearly all the self-deprecating comics are the *writers* (source) of their humor, which thus allows them to transcend while in the moment of being the self-deprecator.

Woody Allen, Groucho Marx, and Charlie Chaplin all perfected this device. They play the fool but also are the source of the narrative—which allows them to transcend the actual predicament that they depict in their stories. Of course, the narrative in which the fool is really the "wise one" is nothing new; Shakespeare famously used this technique, as did many others in literary history (Brown, 2021).

Self-Deprecating Humor for the Audience

Interestingly, lovers of self-deprecating humor do not simply enjoy the moment of distance between themselves and the target of the humor. This is not a case of aggressive humor as described earlier. Instead, the audience member sees themselves in the plight of the self-deprecating character—but, at the same time, they are also able to distance themselves from their own plight by projecting themselves into the character at hand.

How does the appreciator of this form of humor accept the mistakes of the self-deprecating one without judgment of the comic? How do they resist the temptation to view the comic here as a loser? The self-deprecating humor lover seems to participate in a worldview in which life is viewed as inherently filled with embarrassment, mistakes, and faux pas. They are not surprised that the comic loses their glasses in the attempt to fix a light bulb or that they admit that they are unable to concentrate enough to add three numbers together. The mistakes or errors that the comic admits to making are ones that are perfectly understandable to this person—because they fit in with their core view of life.

That view of life is that it is fraught with difficulties, embarrassments, and imperfections. Stated differently, the person believes that it is inherent in life that one will struggle. Part of this view may be that society demands and requires too much of us—so that imperfections, errors, and embarrassments are to be expected. When the self-deprecator, then, admits to mistakes, they can identify with, empathize with, but also laugh at the predicaments that have occurred. Self-deprecation appears, then, as authentic and revealing of the human condition.

PART II

SPECIAL TOPICS
IN THE STUDY
OF HUMOR

Chapter 7

THE HILARIOUSLY FUNNY

Most of the current psychological research (Aharoni, 2018; Filani, 2017) on comedy and humor is based on responses to *jokes*. The typical experimental paradigm presents a subject with a list of jokes and a rating scale by which they estimate the "funniness" of each of these jokes. Some set of psychological variables, assessed within the subject, is then correlated with their sense of humor as measured by their responses to these jokes.

The chief criticism of this type of research focuses on its generalizability to everyday experience. The telling of jokes is, actually, a very small part of everyday life, and it even represents a small part of one's experience of humor. If you were to ask people what the funniest things they've experienced in their lives were—a particular joke would rarely appear on that list of nominations. In my own research (Atlas et al., 2015), I have done precisely that—asked subjects to nominate the most hilariously funny things they've experienced—and jokes played a very small part in their nominations.

More typically, what is most funny to people are personal experiences that involve a narrative that develops into an *inside story* that has a personal meaning for them. Most will nominate experiences such as when their friend made a fool of themselves in front of someone they were trying to impress or a silly thought that occurred during church that they shared with a friend, which led to their being unable to control their laughter, despite the serious sermon being delivered. Often a visual image will be at the center of this comedic experience, as in, "I keep thinking about the time when my brother dropped the groceries all over the street." The hilariously funny is almost always of this character, and the laughter one experiences is uncontrollable and overwhelming. "Whenever I think about Mr. Simpson lecturing the class while Johnny was mooning in the corner, I just can't help but crack up." (Please excuse the pun in that case!)

What is the nature of the hilariously funny, though? Why is it that personal situations are almost always recognized as the most profoundly comedic? What is the role of the visual image in these cases? How does the social sharing of these experiences become so prominent such that they become central to very powerful social relationships? It is these questions that will be addressed in this chapter, with a mind to casting light on the nature of the hilariously funny.

Is there a qualitative difference between this category of the hilariously funny and the simply funny? It appears that this is the case. One can attend a comedy club performance and find much of the material to be extremely funny. A sitcom can produce many comedic moments—even ones that are discussed with friends: "Do you remember the time that George, on *Seinfeld*, quit his job, then thought better of it, so he returned to work and pretended that nothing happened? That was hilarious!" At a dinner party, another couple may relate their funny stories, and, indeed, one may be quite taken by them and even compelled to retell those stories to other friends and marvel at how funny they are. Some well-told jokes are even terrific; they are worthy of being told and retold and promote uproarious laughter time and time again.

But the really hilariously funny rarely comes from one of those domains and, instead, nearly always originates from one's own private experience. The "inside joke" or "family joke" is one form in which this may arise. They are situational, private, and much of the humor may lie in the personalities and idiosyncrasies of the people involved. You had to know Mr. Simpson—how stern he was and how he tortured the class all semester about not being serious enough—to appreciate how funny the gesture of this student was. "You had to be there" is the expression commonly resorted to, especially when others do not share in the experience.

Key Elements of the Hilariously Funny

An Italian family from Boston would head off to Cape Cod for their typical family vacation every summer. The aging matriarch of the family insisted on preparing all their favorite foods to bring with them to be cooked on the Cape. In fact, she was so attached to her spaghetti sauce, prepared over several hours of simmering and using only the finest ingredients, that she would not allow anyone else to touch her sauce on the trip. She held the pot of sauce on her lap, in the passenger seat, while the white-haired patriarch drove. On the highway, an incident occurred when the car in front of them paused and then stopped, forcing the driver to step on the brakes. He did so carefully because he knew that everyone was holding on to something of importance in the car, and the grandkids were in the back. But the car behind him could not stop abruptly and plowed into their car with a sudden jar. The spaghetti sauce went flying, covering everyone and the whole interior of the car with the red sauce. They pulled over, and a police car entered the scene. The officer came to investigate. "We have a major catastrophe here. Looks like everyone in this car is a casualty," he said, noting the prominence of blood on all the passengers. Of course, nobody was seriously injured, but this became the "family joke" for dozens of years to come. (Source who chose anonymity)

This story has all the key elements of good humor: a set of preconditions that are quirky but understandable, a twist of fortune that is frightening but not overwhelming, a misunderstanding by an authority figure, and a resolution that assures no serious consequences. The grandmother's concern with her spaghetti sauce is the key precondition for all further action. Holding the sauce on her own lap is unusual but understandable, given the attachment and reverence she has for her own creation. The accident is the unexpected twist, and the policeman coming to examine the scene then becomes the central feature of comedic action. In fact, it is the policeman's conclusion that all passengers must be severely injured that serves as the central moment of this comedic story. When family members recall this event with hilarious laughter, what they think of is the policeman, arriving on the scene, drawing such a conclusion! Of course, it would not be funny if there were, in fact, serious injuries, but it was just a fender bender that resulted in only minor repairs needed.

This type of story is almost prototypical for the kind of hilariously funny insider story that we enter into and which provides us with the most powerful form of laughter. The question, then, is why are experiences of this sort so powerful and productive in terms of comedy and humor? Three aspects appear to play roles in the hilariously funny experience phenomena. One aspect that appears to play a prominent role is inherent in the question: They are *experiences*. They are not stories told by an outsider. Instead, they refer to living experiences, and those who are present to them seem to find them the funniest. Another aspect is the *visual or frozen* moment within the story. The laughter usually refers back to one moment in time that is the height of comedy—that central moment of the policeman investigating the scene, in this case. Teenagers will remark, "Remember the look on Father McCade's face when Robert came running into class, late, with mud all over him?" That one visual moment plays a prominent role in the hilariously funny comedic experience.

The *social factor* is the final component that appears to be critical in the hilariously funny. One rarely finds that these *moments* are enjoyed alone. Much has been written about the social aspect of humor and laughter (Devereux & Ginsburg, 2001); we laugh more when we see the same comedy film with others than we do when watching alone, and most of our laughter occurs in the presence of and is shared with others. In the case of the hilariously funny, the one who enjoys the scene is usually joined by another who is a corecipient of the comedic vision. Friends or family members are, by far, the most likely coconspirators in the experience (Atlas, et al., 2015). In fact, the laughter is often contagious, and, once one finds the scene incredibly funny, this increases the intensity of the laughter for the other. Finally, the "insider" dimension seems to add to the specialness of this type of comedic experience. One of my own personal experiences may serve to illustrate some of these components in the hilariously funny:

> I was looking for the Sunday *New York Times* at a store in a resort town. When I found that the store I was in did not carry the *Times*, I returned to my rental car and contemplated my next move. I would try another store, a couple of miles down the road. There were some unfamiliar things in the passenger seat of my car, though. Oh, my God—I got into the wrong car! I mistook this other white car for my rental car and was about to try to start the car. I jumped out of that car, for fear of being seen as I had entered the wrong car. I found my car, just behind the "wrong one," jumped in, and took off for the convenience store down the road to look for the *Times*. Much to my delight, they did carry the *Times*, and I grabbed one and headed to the cashier—but now I realized I didn't have my wallet. I'd left my wallet in that other car, back down the road! I don't believe I ever drove more quickly than I did to get back to the first store and the car I had left the wallet in. When I arrived, there were two gentlemen in the car, and I started to explain what happened. They just handed me the wallet, with no expression whatsoever, and I lived happily ever after.

Many of the same components are present in this tale—a simple but quirky precondition, (looking for a newspaper in a store), a couple of twists (getting in the wrong car and leaving one's own wallet in said car), and a benign ending. But notice that the focus in this hilarious story is on one's own mistakes in judgment—thinking another car is your rental and then leaving your wallet before exiting the vehicle. This story, then, becomes one of self-deprecation and embarrassment. How do I explain to these gentlemen that I, mistakenly, left my own wallet in their car? There are three central moments here: 1) realizing that I am not in my own car but someone else's, 2) at the second store when I attempt to pay for the newspaper and realize that I don't have my wallet, and 3) pulling up to the car in which I left the wallet and seeing two men inside, about to leave the spot. Again, the visual images play a large part in promoting the hilarious laughter that my family has enjoyed since this event took place.

Many of the hilariously funny scenes that people report are of an even more primitive and simple nature:

> "We were trying to 'sneak-eat' Twinkies during church and the creamy center erupted and hit Mrs. Kamp right in the face!"

> "We were playing Ping-Pong in our basement with the windows open and a bird flew in right at my friend's head!"

> (Fictional narratives)

The image of the old woman with Twinkie cream on her face in church is enough to bring on uncontrollable laughter whenever these two friends reminisce. And the look of surprise on the Ping-Pong player's face as the bird approaches his friend in the basement evokes the same type of hilarity for them.

Let's look at the components of hilarious laughter again with an eye on the phenomenological experience to illuminate its character more fully. We might start with the affective component, which is concerned with a person's emotional reaction, because this is at the heart of the experience. Is this kind of laughter really distinct from other forms? It appears so. First, the laughter here manifests itself in a more explosive, full-bodied way and much quicker than we find with other humor. We go from zero to 70 in a moment's time. This is why language such as "laughter *erupted*" or "we *burst* into laughter" is so prevalent in this domain.

But the experience of this sort of laughter is worth taking note of. Laughing hysterically is a very powerful experience, to say the least. It overwhelms all previous moods and is often described as a cleansing feeling. No bad mood can survive hilarious laughter. If one is depressed—of course, they are less likely to engage in hilarious laughter, but if they manage to enter into the state of such—their previous mood is erased. Perhaps this is why we often attempt to "cheer people up" with a funny story or tale. But literally nothing can approach the power of this extreme laughter for eradicating a bad mood.

Part of the reason for the power of this kind of laughter is that it is, inherently, involuntary. One becomes possessed by the image, and the laughter erupts without any volition on the part of the person. We are captured by it. In fact, this is seen in the attempts people make to control their state—grabbing their belly, holding their head in their hands, or trying to straighten up their posture after they've slumped to the floor. Hilarious laughter actually "knocks you out" and often leads to a collapse onto the floor. Efforts to control one's state then often ensue, and normality is resumed if those efforts are successful. Interestingly, though, there is generally a feeling of disappointment once normality resumes. What, then, is this state of hilarious laughter that is so powerful?

After a laughing fit of some duration, one is exhausted and often feels *cleansed*. In fact, one of the common phrases used here is, "I almost died laughing." Of course, much has been written about the healing power of comedy, humor, and laughter (Cousins, 1979; Savage et al., 2017), but little distinction has been made between the mildly amusing and the hilariously funny. I would propose that the full-bodied belly laugh that erupts in the case of the latter is much more "healing" and "healthy" than a little chuckle. One can even notice one's breathing improving, one's sinuses cleared, and a much more positive outlook ensuing following an extreme laughter experience. This, too, says nothing about the social dynamic and the strength of social bonding that occurs with the shared experience of this kind of laughter.

> I laughed so hard I thought I was gonna die. Then I looked at you and you were collapsed on the floor laughing, too. That made me laugh even harder, and I was gasping for breath. Oh, my God, was that a release! I slept really well that night. (fictional vignette)

Depth and Meaning of the Hilariously Funny

There is a kind of *sanctity* to both the experience of laughter of this sort and the stories that provoke it. It is almost as if these stories and their (usually shared) experience as hilariously funny carry a spiritual significance. The stories take on the role of the mythic, providing an archetypal message that is conveyed through the telling of the tale and the laughter a kind of evidential validity of their truth. The transcendence reached in the extreme laughter is enough to "wipe away the world" and allow one to reach beyond and achieve freedom from one's troubles. In the social context, that insider-hilarious-story allows a couple to bond in an "us against the world" sort of stance. It is as if they share an "inside story" that the rest of the world could not possibly understand or share.

What is the *meaning* of these hilarious stories, though? Are there any common themes? One that emerges quite prominently is that rebellious, anti-authority position in which the laughers gain a kind of revenge against their authoritarian tormenters. In the case of a prank, this may represent a "taking down" of the authority as they demonstrated the vulnerability of a disliked authority. Many of the hilarious stories of children do, indeed, involve parents, teachers, or other authorities whose power is ordinarily felt as limiting and dehumanizing. In the prank or the incident that is hilarious, children are able to overcome that authority—at least for one brief moment and, sharing that inside joke, take solace in the known freedom they experience in that shared incident. Here's another silly personal experience that may serve to illustrate this kind of shared inside humor, which we would categorize in the hilariously funny genre:

> When I was about 12 years old, my friend and I wanted to go out bicycle riding in the evening. We'd heard about the new law that stated you must have a light on your bicycle if you are riding at night. So, we taped a flashlight onto the bike, but it wasn't really working well and was constantly in the process of falling off the bike. As we were riding, we turned into a shopping center to better secure the flashlight and some police cars, lights flashing, pulled into the lot at the same time. The cops jumped out of their cars, drew their guns, and shouted, "Alright, put your hands over your heads; you're under arrest!" My friend and I thought we were under arrest for driving with an ineffective bicycle light. Of course, the police were talking to some "real criminals" they had pulled over. We have always found that incident extremely funny, ever since.

The idea that we could be pulled over and confronted by an armed policeman, at gunpoint, for having a taped bicycle light is just hilarious! Of course, a large part of the humor here is the sharing of that story between friends. We have both, undoubtedly, told that story to dozens of people over the years, but nobody will enjoy it at the level we do when we are together.

Why, though, is the social dimension so crucial to the hilariously funny category of experience? Can one have a solitary joke, situation, or memory that still has the intensity and power of the hilariously funny? From my own research study, it appears that this is not possible; when subjects are asked to nominate the most hilariously funny experiences they've encountered, none present solitary examples. The social element of this experience seems to be integral to the experience. This, moreover, is the key to answering the question posed here. What is being laughed at is not simply the situation or the object that is being considered. In fact, the emphasis is not on the object but on the human condition that is shared between those who share the comedic experience. The laughter itself is in the joint recognition of a kind of universal truth.

> The priest stops in the middle of his sermon and pulls out a large handkerchief and slowly brings it up to his face. We then hear a loud "honking" as he blows his nose. The noise is prominent and wild—but the priest then returns to the sermon as if nothing happened, with the same serious tone as before. Children in the back look at each other and start giggling uncontrollably. (fictional narrative)

It is clear, in this case, what the children who laugh at the preacher's blowing his nose during the sermon are laughing at. How loud! How crude! And, of course, we know that humor is so often based on *contrast* and, in this case, the contrast of the honking sound with the serious tone of the sermon is what "gets us." What adds to the hilariousness is that the priest does not acknowledge this contrast and goes on with the very serious speech as if nothing happened.

The Social Component in the Hilariously Funny

The children giggle at the time and then erupt with laughter later on, recalling their experience as the preacher reaches into his pocket, pulls out his handkerchief, slowly assembles it in position, and then belts out a honk as he blows his nose into the handkerchief. They reexperience it together, later, and "crack up" uncontrollably—as they take turns mimicking the preacher's motion, sound, and, most important, demeanor. What is perhaps funniest is the preacher's attempt to remain serious, contemplative, and religious as this bodily function is prominently expressed and the loud sound of "honking" erupts in a way that, clearly, belies the serious, religious framework. There is no denying the body. That is what is "seen" by the children—which, in fact, is quite a powerful, universal truth. But it is not nearly as funny without the *shared* perception. They become one vision—looking at the preacher and united in their vision of the truth—and tickled by it. What allows them to laugh at this truth, though, rather than be humbled by it or consider it contemplatively?

It is their alienation or separation from the authority, their childishness, and their otherness from the preacher's reality that surely plays a prominent role here. The preacher can be laughed at because he is *other*—and also because of his "claim" that the religious can defeat, overcome, and relegate the body irrelevant. But the children know better. They see the preacher's being inside of a claim and are transcendent to it, in a very basic and primitive way. This is also why children's laughter—at an adult—can be so painful and hurtful for the adult; children's laughter is a laughter of knowledge of a certain sort. What the preacher takes as *serious* is not really as important as that preacher claims it to be.

But to return to the social aspects of the hilariously funny, we can see that this church giggle and subsequent shared eruption of laughter would not exist without the partner. Just like the proverbial "if a tree falls in the forest and nobody is there to hear it, does it make a sound?" question, we can ask if something funny happens, but nobody is there to share it with you, is it still funny? Suppose you're unaccompanied in the church. Though you find the honking funny, you contain any impulse to actually laugh. Later on, during the informal reception, you feel a need to engage another in the question, "Did you find it funny when the priest blew his nose so loudly in the middle of the sermon?" If you find that willing partner, you can then engage in laughter. If not, the hilariously funny is stymied.

The child has to look at their friend and giggle together to begin the process. Indeed, the social dimension nearly overwhelms the power of the content; over time, it surely does. In hilarious, overwhelming laughter, it is common, for example, for people to remark that "I can't even remember what we're laughing at." The laughter is contagious and feeds on the social dimension, taking on a life of its own.

What is that social dimension to which we keep referring? What is it that the person sees in the other, as the other is "cracking up," that allows them to let loose, uncontrollably? Some of our answers are already present in the language we use to describe such incidents. "Cracking up" is clearly a reference to a letting go of one's usual state of mind. "I just fell apart" or "I lost it" are other commonly used phrases here. What does one lose, though, or what cracks? The hints that these phrases provide lead us to a very grand-scale weakening of our ordinary sense of self and world. To "lose it" means to let go of one's usual framework of self/world in a way that allows one to see things in a totally different manner. The seriousness of the church service, for example, is truly ruptured by the letting go that is manifest in the children's laughing at the honking sound of the preacher blowing his nose.

The truth is, of course, that the serious worldview in which the preacher is absolutely revered is already ruptured. The children already look askance at this "seriously religious view" that is being espoused—which is what allows the giddiness to occur at all. But the honking sound allows that structure to be fully broken open for the children. How, then, does the looking of the other play a role in this? What is seen in the other? The other's letting go is what allows the person to also let go; there is a kind of mutual recognition of the crevice that serves to facilitate the complete breakdown of ordinary consciousness.

As we utter these phrases, it sounds almost as if the hilariously funny is almost a kind of mystical experience. The hilariously funny, indeed, has many characteristics of such. In fact, many hold these experiences as precious in ways that one might consider a religious or mystical experience; they are cherished, preserved, and told and retold repeatedly. Never, however, do they reach the level or magnitude that they had in their original moment. As already mentioned, often others who are outside of the original social group are unable to appreciate the power or degree of humor that one experienced, and still does, upon recall of these hilariously funny experiences. All of this, in fact, speaks to the special standing that this category holds for us and allows for this comparison with the divine.

Characteristics of Those Who Enjoy the Hilariously Funny

Since this is a new category that is being proposed here, we cannot rely on research to help us identify those characteristics that would play a role in the enjoyment of the hilariously funny. It seems, on the other hand, that some folks are simply more *ready* to engage is this level of humor than others. If we take the converse—those who could not possibly enter into hilarious laughter—we can see the central factor here fairly easily. A person who is very self-controlled and cautious would generally not allow themselves to be taken by the hilariously funny. They would experience that kind of laughter and release as a rupture that is too threatening to their ability to maintain self-control. On the contrary, those who embrace the hilariously funny would seek out those memories and experiences that would facilitate this form and level of laughter. I suppose one can imagine an interesting dynamic that would ensue as these types encounter each other—one seeking that release and the other protecting against it.

Chapter 8

PARALINGUAL ASPECTS OF HUMOR

Paralingual aspects of humor would include everything that lies outside of the *actual* content of humor. Some of those aspects—delivery, timing, appearance, body gestures, and so forth—have long been considered critical from the standpoint of the performance of comedy. The stand-up comic, for example, hones their craft by incorporating voices, gestures, and facial expressions into their act. Paralingual factors play a large role, however, in virtually all comedy. In this chapter, we consider some of these critical aspects of humor.

Delivery

A new inmate entered the prison and settled into his cell. Everything was as he expected; there were tough guys and little freedom. At night, once the bedtime check was completed, he noticed that a strange practice went on. One inmate would call out a number—34 or 52 or 78, for example—after each of which all the other inmates would start laughing. Each night, some inmate called out a series of numbers, and the other inmates laughed hysterically. After a few nights of this, the new inmate had to know what was going on, so he approached another inmate during the afternoon work session. "What is this calling of numbers, followed by laughter?"

The other inmate explained, "We've all been in here for so long that we all know each other's jokes by now. So we just numbered them all so we don't have to repeat the whole joke. We have exactly 145 jokes now numbered."

"Ah," said the new inmate. "I get it. I'll have to learn the numbered jokes."

"Sure," said the other inmate. "I'll give you the list after you've been here a month."

But the new inmate decided to conduct a little test the following night. After everyone had settled into their cells and the lights were out, he began calling out numbers, "42, then 37, 86, 63." He noticed, though, that there was no laughter from the other inmates. He tried again, "54. 91." Still, no laughter. So, the next day he approached this same confidante to find out what happened. "Hey, didn't you hear me call out the numbered jokes last night?"

The friend nodded his head affirmatively.

"What happened? Why didn't anyone laugh?"

The friend looked him straight in the eye and explained, "Bad delivery!" (Upjoke, 2020)

The delivery of jokes has long been recognized as a key factor in humor. So, too, in "funny situations," the paralingual aspects are far more important than one might expect. "It was the way he looked at me that just cracked me up" is a common exclamation. In fact, the paralingual aspects of humor are so important that one has to wonder whether the whole enterprise here, which is of a distinctly lingual nature, can really capture or illuminate humor. Humor is truly one of those things that must be experienced in real time and space, and much is lost as one talks about or—even worse, reads about—humor. But still, we continue.

Timing

What aspects of delivery are important? Why is humor so dependent on these paralingual aspects? One factor that has received a great deal of attention is that ineffable concept of *timing*. Timing refers, mainly, to appropriate pauses prior to delivering the punchlines. Comedians often talk about making sure they do not rush their jokes so that people miss the punch. In professional singing, there is a similar concept of "phrasing" where singers express meaning more powerfully by grouping phrases that hang together and developing sufficient separation and distinction for each phrase. Cognitive psychologists tell us that we process information in "chunks" or units.

But timing in humor refers to both the process of phrasing and also, literally, pausing long enough for people to process the information efficiently and, finally, highlighting the punchline by giving it sufficient distinction from the lead-in to the punchline. In the earlier example, one must pause before and then emphasize the key line "bad delivery." Much has been written about the importance of timing in comedy, and potential stand-up comedians are taught to work on timing as they develop their craft.

Interestingly, though, two researchers recently investigated some of the classic aspects of comedic timing in the laboratory (Attardo & Pickering, 2011). They studied joke-telling to determine if rate of speech differed for the setup as opposed to the punchline. They also looked at the classic "pause" prior to the punchline but found no evidence for either of these "folk theories" that have long been advanced about timing in comedy. There were no differences in speech rate between the setup and punchline and no clear "pregnant pause" preceding the climax of the joke. Attardo and Pickering conclude that "we ... have strong evidence that the folk-theory of pausological marking of punch lines is false." (p. 246)

The mechanisms underlying comedic timing, then, have not been established empirically. Experientially, though, bad timing can clearly destroy comedy or lead to less laughter. If, for example, the audience is not clear about what the punchline is or the second joke is begun before the audience is allowed to fully enjoy the laugh from the previous joke, the comedian's success is surely compromised. Attardo and Pickering admit that timing may involve even more subtle aspects such as voice pitch or even volume—which would, presumably, emphasize the punchline over and above the setup of the joke. But we also must consider that sometimes a bad joke is just not funny regardless of the timing of delivery and, perhaps, a good joke works reasonably well regardless of the delivery.

Appearance

Of course, the appearance of a comic plays a role in the audience's experience of that comedian. Some comedians, like Jerry Seinfeld or Jay Leno, are "ordinary looking," which becomes a kind of obstacle in trying to entertain people. Others have a strange or unusual appearance or wear a facial expression, like a cynical sneer, that provides effective comedic inspiration. Comedy is aided by an offbeat, out-of-the ordinary, "silly" appearance such as Red Skelton or even Sam Kinison's very goofy "look." When you think of that expression, "It's hard to take him seriously," it is applicable; a goofy, silly appearance is easy to laugh at and hard to ignore. An appearance that represents the out of the ordinary, the strange, and the *offbeat* is a distinct advantage for the comic. Humor thrives on the offbeat and not on the regular, ordinary, conservative, and normal.

The fact that we even use an expression such as "funny-looking" for those creatures or objects that are not regular indicates the connection between the irregular and humor. One could laugh simply at the way someone or something, perhaps an animal, looks. Of course, simply looking unusual would not be humorous; the Elephant Man is hardly comedic. What is required is that the appearance is "goofy" or "off" or somehow silly. Youth may play a role here as well, since goofy-looking children are particularly humorous. The key seems to be that the unusualness is innocuous—not something serious that may involve a disease process or a debilitating physical disability.

Many comedians have the advantage of that goofy, silly appearance, which allows them fan support almost immediately and intuitively. Others, like Steve Martin (2008), worked on his presentation and added props so that he would appear particularly funny-looking. A funny appearance, however, does not seem to guarantee success, nor does the lack of it absolutely rule out success. Jerry Seinfeld and Jon Stewart are good examples of comedians who are relatively ordinary looking but still became major stars—but mostly through their comedic minds rather than on the basis of physical attributes.

Body Gestures

How do bodily postures and gestures affect comedic expression? "I love the way he moves!" is a common comment of those who like a comedian. Without exploring all the nuances of body movement and the specific effectiveness of certain gestures, it is easy to see that flexible and unusual movements are a large part of bodily humor. The comedian does not have to be a contortionist, but their ability to move in a smooth, efficient manner goes a long way in humor. Watch Bill Cosby's (2007) depiction of a drunken man, with the one leg still while the other moves freely. Dick Van Dyke's agility in contorting his body was one of the key factors in his show's success. Both Groucho Marx and Charlie Chaplin, even before them, were masters of comedic movement.

This flexibility of movement serves as a way of representing "goofiness" or "silliness" within movement. It says, "I don't take myself seriously," whereas the opposite—rigidity—connotes narrowmindedness and seriousness. In fact, the foil of jokes in the Marx Brothers movies, for example, were always people who held high positions and held their bodies in very rigid postures. Margaret

Dumont, the most prominent foil, would hold her head up high and her body rigid as she made her declarations and stated her "high society" opinions. She would attempt to scold Groucho by rigidly pointing her finger and demanding that he take her needs seriously. Flexibility of movement, on the other hand, seems to signify a kind of freedom—a fun-loving attitude that is so important in humor.

What about the sheer *speed of movement*? Humor is often connected with high levels of speed. Think of Robin Williams, who moved and talked with a lightning-fast pace, often overwhelming the audience and making them laugh as a result. Sometimes— often, in fact—one does not even know what they heard, but the speed with which Williams delivered his lines is funny in itself. In physical humor, actions often occur so rapidly that the recognition of their consequences is nearly impossible, at the moment of action. When that recognition takes place, a humorous situation has emerged before you could take stock of what was happening. In *The Three Stooges*, for example, the recipient of a blow often is depicted as "not even knowing what hit him" even after the hit has occurred. He then, slowly, becomes aware of the hit and the consequences (e.g., falling down) begin. A slow, steady pace, on the other hand, is generally not funny. Slow and steady connotes serious, laborious, and staid.

> All preparations for the trip to hospital have been completed. Dick Van Dyke is ready. Laura is pregnant and overdue; she'll be "ready to go" at any moment now. When the signal comes that they need to head to the hospital, though, he freaks out, grabbing all the wrong things and forgetting to put his pants on. His movements are herky-jerky, wild and crazy. (Reiner, 1962)

Rushing is, in itself, humorous. In the process of rushing, one loses oneself; planful behavior gives way to instinctive, more primitive behavior. This can lead to forgetting the most important aspects of life and doing things that are completely tangential to the planned intention. When rushing, movements are not smooth and precise, but rather, choppy and strange. This incites humor as the ordinary parameters are abandoned in favor of the revelation of the baser and more primitive—a common theme of comedy.

Anger and Screaming in Comedy

Anger and screaming are also used, quite commonly, in humor. The comic Sam Kinison made screaming his signature form of entertaining. He uses a screaming voice, among other voices, to provide strong emphasis. For example, he claims that, if one had the strength, they could break up with someone by screaming at the top of their lungs, "Oh, would you get out of my life! You make it hell!" (Kinison, 1986) The basic approach he uses is based on an angry and hostile view—which was very much appreciated by his audience. Without the screaming tone, he would probably not have been nearly as effective. In recent years, this approach to comedy has become increasingly popular.

How does the anger of the comedian provide comic relief for the audience? First, it is clear that the audience likes and appreciates the screaming, angry tone of these comedians, because laughter arises precisely after each scream from the comic. The audience member is able to live that anger, experience it—without having it within them or living with the consequences of being that angry. They get the benefits without the usual consequences—stress, conflict, and anxiety. It is a fairly classic case of *vicarious experience*. Of course, they must have such a need or, in other words, have the anger within them in some fashion, but when Kinison yells and screams or Lewis Black (2016) expresses his anger, they are both inside and outside of that anger—inside enough to experience it but outside enough to avoid the accompanying consequences that usually ensue.

Use of Voices

Another very common comedic tool is the imitation of a variety of voices. This can come in the form of actual impersonation of real celebrities or simply in the employment of a multitude of voices in telling a comedic story. The comic may utilize the voice of a lover, a parent, a teacher—none of whom are people the audience knows but they become reified in the narrative. Of course, most commonly, the voice is portrayed as a caricature of the real person. For example, a mother may be portrayed with an especially whiney, harsh voice that provides some of the comedic power within the story. In my own life as a teacher, I found that using voices of various fictitious characters was a technique that provided entertainment and excitement in the classroom—even though I had virtually no talent as an impersonator. It served the purpose of bringing the various characters we were discussing "to life" and allowed the students to experience a more full-bodied narrative at the same time that it freed their perception of the teacher from that of a single mode of presentation or a single perspective.

Facial Expressions

> A lot of people ask me: how do you manage to contort your face in such crazy ways? I never know how to answer that question. (Regan, 2017)

Facial expressions are an extremely important paralingual aspect of comedic presentations. Many comedians use exaggerated facial contortions to add color and silliness within their act. One commonly utilized expression is that of surprise or astonishment. Eyes bulge, facial muscles stretch, and wrinkles appear as the comic takes on the look of sheer bewilderment as they describe some aspect of culture or human behavior. This brings the audience into the *mode of humor* to consider the target examined as strange, bizarre, or silly. In fact, it allows the audience to both laugh at the target of the humor but also at the comic themselves.

Of course, we must also mention the opposite extreme, deadpan humor, in which the comic displays no expression whatsoever, with a similar result. The unaffected face of the deadpan comic in the presence of the bizarre and irrational content that they are discussing is also, by contrast, humorous. Deadpan humor will be examined with more depth in chapter 11, which focuses on Incongruity and Discrepancy humor.

Mood in Humor

The discussion of the use of anger in comedy could be seen as part of a larger discussion of the use of mood in humor. Comedians pay a lot of attention to "setting the mood" in their performances—making sure that they have a positive, striking, and powerful entrance. A well-tested first joke allows the audience to relax and share a positive mood with the comic. Steve Martin (2008) devoted a great deal of energy to finding the best opening lines when he was a stand-up comic. He continued to study other comedian's opening lines and particularly loved Sam Kinison's, which he felt "set the mood" so well for Kinison's wild and irreverent humor.

> I saw him (Sam Kinison) at the Comedy Store in Beverly Hills. And he came on—it was comedian after comedian after comedian. And he came on and he said, you've seen a lot of comedians here tonight. Some really good, some, you know, nice, OK. But there's a difference between them and me. Them, you might want to see again sometime. (Martin, 2008)

Similarly, comedic movies often begin with a major comedic twist that sets the tone for a comedic atmosphere throughout the movie. When a movie begins, one is often wondering how seriously one should "take" the movie. Once the audience detects that this is, clearly, a wild and crazy comedy, it sets a comedic mood in which they can let go and enjoy it as a comedy without taking the movie and plot too seriously.

Research on the effects of mood on nearly every facet of human life would indicate that a positive mood is likely to lead to more laughter, enjoyment, and engagement in humor (Wicker, et al., 1981; Yoon, 2018). The mood induction procedure, however, could vary from presenting a smiling, positive attitude to a deadpan or even angry tone that is somehow playful at the same time. In fact, the concept of *play* may be quite central here, as it is juxtaposed with that of a serious, sober, or straightforward approach to life—all of which are not conducive to a humorous atmosphere. The playful tone can be communicated through a variety of methods, but the key is to establish a lighthearted mood that allows the audience to loosen their hold on their usual mode of being and enjoy the humor that follows.

Funny Words

The pure sound of some words lend themselves to humor. The word "mashed" is funnier than "blended" so, when Woody Allen says, "I'll have the alfalfa sprouts and the mashed yeast" in *Annie Hall* (1977), it is a more powerful and humorous poke at the health food movement in California in the 1970s than if he had used a word like "blended." Research (Westbury et al., 2019) has examined the effect that unusual and unexpected words have on humor ratings, concluding that both factors play a major role in the experience of humor.

Also, words that are not even words, such as those used in children's nursery rhymes and in other "silly humor" (Seed, 2015) can provide a humorous effect. Seed gives the example of "ognib," which is not a word. Certain sounds appear to have humorous characteristics and can be used strategically to amuse because of their odd sounds and, sometimes, surprising placement in sentences. Some have suggested that words that begin with the "k" sound, for example, are inherently funny. If I said that I have a *caboodle* of baseball cards it would be funnier than simply saying that I have an assemblage of such cards.

Food, Music, and Drugs

There is much wisdom in the Las Vegas nightclub scene in which one is provided food, beverage, and often music to set the scene for the comedian. The psychologist Alice Isen (1987) demonstrated repeatedly, in the lab, something that virtually everyone already knew intuitively—that food serves as a mood enhancer. So many commonly used sayings, such as "the key to a person's heart is through their stomach," had emphasized the same point. Whether we take an evolutionary, neurological, or social psychological perspective to the phenomenon, we come to the same conclusion: Eating breeds better moods! Would any comedian or comic actor or producer want their audience to enter one of their performances on an empty stomach that is growling with hunger? Food, on the other hand, may be a necessary but not sufficient condition for the enjoyment of humor. It still must be funny!

Music has been utilized alongside comedy for many years. One striking example here would be the silent films of the early 20th century. They were not silent, in fact, but filled with music to enhance the atmosphere, the suspense, and the humor involved in the film. The Marx Brothers used musical interludes (Harpo playing the harp) as a kind of mood enhancer in most of their movies.

This could be the subject of a whole work unto itself—the connection between music and humor. In fact, a recent work (Evans & Hayward, 2016) has attempted to address the connections between sound and comedy in a historical manner. Some trends, however, can be identified here to begin such an investigation. Music is often used in film to enhance a comedic scene or to provide clues for the audience to view a scene in a comedic manner. The music itself primes the audience to perceive the scene within a humorous mode.

An excerpt from Allan Sherman's (1963) "Hello Muddah, Hello Faddah (A Letter From Camp)" song illustrates the way that rhyming lyrics, combined with music, can provide hilarious humor. "Hello Muddah, hello Faddah. Here I am at Camp Grenada. Camp is very entertaining, and they say we'll have some fun if it stops raining."

Many comedians, in fact, have used music as a part of their performances. Steve Martin, Allan Sherman, Steve Allen, and Steven Wright come immediately to mind, but there are hundreds of comedians who have utilized music within their comedic work. Silly lyrics often accompany familiar songs that are transformed into humorous pieces. Even the psychologist Albert Ellis used cute, musical lyrics and his rather unpleasant (but funny) singing voice to amuse listeners and also help them grasp the principles of Rational Emotive Behavior Therapy (Ellis & MacLaren, 1998).

What is it, though, about music that inspires comedy? One could easily settle for an answer that would point to mood as the key factor in the equation. Music inspires and enhances positive moods, and positive moods, in turn, facilitate humor. But many things, like sex, lead to good moods but do not lead to comedic reactions, for the most part. The sing-songy, rhythmic quality of music, on the other hand, lends itself to humor as does the rhyming within the lyrics. Rhyming expresses a form of language humor in which many of the elements of humor reside—contrast, surprise, and multiple meanings. Waiters and alligators have little in common, as do sissies and Ulysses, but Sherman's lyrics point out—quite surprisingly—how concepts that are quite disparate can be placed side by side in a rhyming, sing-songy tune that provokes a chuckle.

We have only to visit a bar or saloon to see the immediate connection between humor and the use of alcohol. Three friends enter the bar, looking fairly grim from a tough day at the office. They are shaking their heads, saying, "I need a drink!" After a couple of drinks have been consumed, we hear lots of joking and laughing among these friends—and perhaps even the involvement of other patrons in a bawdy, rowdy conversation that involves a great deal of humor.

> If the whole world smoked a joint at the same time, there would be world peace for at least two hours. Followed by a global food shortage.
>
> Q: What is Reality?
> A: An illusion caused by a lack of good weed.
>
> Q: How many Stoners does it take to change a light bulb?
> A: Who cares, man; it's too bright in here anyway!
> (Jokes4us, 2021)

Marijuana is notoriously tied to humor in a multitude of ways. Many people report their first experiences of getting high on pot as being dominated by "the giggles" or laughing hysterically at things that aren't normally funny at all. Drugs that alter one's sense of reality can easily be tied to comedic experiences, as the recognition that one is not viewing the world in the ordinary way but in some unusual other way can be experienced as humorous. That humor, moreover, is likely to be contagious, as your friends are also having similar experiences and you share that "otherworldly" experience with others. Some describe this as akin to having an "inside joke" with their friends in that they are having this common experience that is quite out of the ordinary. "Getting high" (a common way of capturing the effects of marijuana) also generally involves a positive, high mood—which, again, has been found to be an inspiration for comedy.

With drugs like marijuana, moreover, the notion of *transcendence* becomes more prominent, since one can often feel that they are "above it all" or free from the normal constraints of reality. That kind of transcendence may or may not involve a comedic experience, however. Given the power of food, drugs, and music to induce positive moods and humor, one can see why the Las Vegas experience of dinner followed by an opening act of a singer and the main act of a comedian, coupled with a few cocktails, has been such a winning formula!

Chapter 9

BEING LAUGHED AT

There is a body of literature that is focused on the psycho-pathological aspects of the fear of being laughed at. This disorder, which is not an officially recognized one, has been called "gelotophobia" (Stephens, 2014), and the humor scholar Willibald Ruch (1998) has conducted a good deal of research on this disorder. Technically, this would be considered by mental health practitioners as a *simple phobia* (American Psychiatric Association, 2013) but, in fact, there is nothing simple about it. Those who experience gelotophobia tend to have emotions such as fear, shame, and anger when confronted with a situation in which they feel that they are being laughed at. There are behavioral consequences as well; those suffering from this simple phobia tend to avoid social situations as much as possible, for example.

But the present concern is not with defining this disorder, but with the experience and fear of being laughed at. If our primary question is, "What is humor?" or "What is it to laugh?" then one avenue for investigation of that question is to look at the experience of *being laughed at* as an inroad to our primary question. Both are human forms and are viewed here in a phenomenological manner. Being laughed at is a powerful, almost primordial fear for human beings. One could even argue that much motivation derives from the attempt to avoid such an encounter or at least a perceived encounter. For example, people often talk about the fear of being laughed at or ridiculed by their parents as a driving force in their push for success.

Once successful, many people utter statements about their peers like, "Well, maybe they're not laughing at me anymore." Note that empirical work on gelotophobia has not addressed this *perception* that others might be laughing at you nearly as much as the actual experience of being laughed at. This is one of those experiences, however, which rarely actually occurs but about which we spend a great deal of time and energy worrying. In other words, it is a rare case, indeed, that people literally laugh at us, but we tend to concern ourselves with the possibility of being laughed at quite a bit.

What is it, then, to be laughed at? Why is this such a primary concern when it so rarely actually occurs?

> I was on the bus, heading home from school, when I noticed that nobody seemed to want to sit next to me anymore. Usually, if I got on early, someone would eventually sit next to me, but this time everyone seemed to be shying away from me. After a while, I noticed that two groups of kids were pointing at me at various points and giggling, "You see what I mean?" "Yeah, it's definitely there," and more laughter would occur after each pointing and statement took place. I felt like dying. I would have rather been dead. I felt like I stood out and was seen but wished I wasn't there at all. It was horrible! (fictional vignette)

This is something like the primordial "being laughed at" experience—peers are seeing you as funny-looking or just plain ugly and sharing a laugh at your expense. Can one ever recover completely from such an experience? Many of us can point to such an experience and perhaps feel that we can never fully recover from such an awful adolescent experience.

But what is so terrible about being laughed at? Notice that, in the experience described above, *nothing actually occurred* in a physical manner that would directly threaten the victim. The person was not hurt or hit in any way. The perpetrators were simply looking and pointing. Of course, pointing at a person is a very powerful and painful "attack" of a sort. But no physical or even verbal abuse was given in this story. The target, also, was not rejected from a desired social group, although the laughter may have intimated that sort of outcome to the victim. Yet they were a victim of something that seems far worse than even being beaten up or attacked physically.

The Exposure Involved in Being Laughed At

So, what is the pain of being laughed at? It is the pain of being seen as inside from outside. The victim must somehow believe that they are being *exposed*. "They are seeing me as ugly, stupid, limited—or just plain nothing." Now, we should probably make a distinction between being laughed at when one is completely secure with one-self and the other represents no threat, danger, or power. Of course, this is not traumatic for most people, since any other who holds no particular power is not a threat for "seeing through" the person. In fact, if a person laughs at another and that target simply shrugs it off, it is quite disabling for the perpetrator. But that is probably the rare case. Instead, being laughed at is generally quite debilitating for the victim.

Some people describe the experience of being laughed at as similar to being "seen naked" in a public place. There is no covering, no filter, and no protection from the eye of the other. When one is laughed at, one experiences this melting down of the persona, the covering, the controlled aspects of the self in favor of the essential nothingness that one fears one is. The greater that fear of *being nothing*, the greater the fear of being laughed at.

What is the *devaluing* in being seen naked? It is quite akin to being laughed at. Being seen as naked represents another very primitive fear that many people have. Just think about all the trouble we go to such that this does not happen (clothes, dividers, rules, etc.). But, sometimes, despite all those measures, an exposure occurs. Why is this horrible if nothing substantial or manifest is actually involved? The fear of being exposed is one of our strongest senses of vulnerability.

One strategy for dealing with the horror of being laughed at is to not allow yourself to be seen by others. As people say, when you invest in relationships, you make yourself vulnerable. Of course, what we usually think of when considering this risky self-invest-ment is the fear of rejection. Being laughed at, though, is a form of rejection that can be extremely painful.

> A 12-year-old girl comes home from school. "Mom, all the other kids were laughing at me because of this plaid skirt that I wore. They asked if we now have a uniform because I look like I'm wearing a school uniform. I was so embarrassed!"
>
> The mother is horrified and tries to console the girl. "I think you look great in that outfit! Don't listen to the other kids. What do they know about fashion? Don't worry about it." (fictional vignette)

Of course, it's virtually impossible for the preteen to make use of the mother's advice; the image of the other children laughing at her simply cannot be removed from her mind. In fact, it may be that both the image and the sound of peers laughing at her are perhaps forever imbedded in her mind. How does she overcome this? Is there any cure for this trauma? The mother's advice here is quite sound—the victim should attempt to ignore the judgments of others—but can this be done? For a 12-year-old, this is not a realistic option, at least not immediately.

Laughing at a person is akin to "being outside" of the person and seeing them as inside of something. This is, indeed, one of our basic human fears—that we are inside of something that others can see and we cannot. That is why it is so terrifying to be laughed at by others. It ties in with a very primordial fear—of *being seen*. As one is laughed at, one fears that they are being seen and that there is no chance of eradicating that. The usual reaction is horror and then anger, which sometimes leads to internalization and sometimes to aggressive reactionary action.

> A child prefers to do crossword puzzles during recess rather than play dodgeball. His parents request and are granted the right to allow the child to do that. But the other kids—the mainstream, popular kids—find out about this. They get together at the end of recess, find the kid, and point and laugh at him in unison. The child is flabbergasted, embarrassed, horrified, and angry. (fictional vignette)

The child could internalize this horror by not responding to the other children and trying to forget this ever happened. He may rationalize, telling himself that his tormenters are "just stupid jocks and are never going to go anywhere in life." But, at some level, the damage has been done. He cannot respond anymore, and he was defeated by the other kids. They saw him as inside of something stupid and attacked him on those grounds. He could not defend himself, so he tries to forget it and deny it.

Of course, the child could also respond immediately to the other kids when they laugh at him. "You're just a bunch of idiots. These games actually are more challenging than a stupid game of dodgeball." In this case, he defends himself—but does this work? Generally not, because *laughed at* has an almost overwhelming power. As already stated, the damage has been done before the moment when the victim can either internalize and deny or stay and fight.

The study of being laughed at is important not only because this experience is so terrifying and disabling but also because it reveals, by serving as the converse, what it means to "laugh at." Laughing at is being outside of, transcendent, to the object being looked at as inside. Of course, not all humor is a "laughing at" in the sense of at the expense of others. The object of humor does not need to be another person's folly. But when it is, the target of that humor suffers in a very damaging, powerful manner that is undeniable and difficult to overcome.

Torturers throughout history are often depicted as laughing at their victims as they employ their abusive tactics. The famous character of the Joker, for example, with his hideous evil laugh, depicted as almost involuntary in recent films, displays precisely these characteristics. *Laughing at*, as the converse of being laughed at, is a form of humor that is destructive, vindictive, and dehumanizing.

Chapter 10

HUMOR AND THE NEGATIVE

Larry David, one of the creators of *Seinfeld* and the comedic genius behind *Curb Your Enthusiasm*, was once asked in an interview, "Things are always going wrong for you in your shows. In your own life, do things always go wrong like that or do things sometimes go smoothly without any problems?"

David replied, "Of course things go well—a lot of the time—but when that happens, it's just not very funny." (David, 2016)

What is the connection between humor and the negative? Why is it that humor thrives so much on mistakes, errors, problems, and even sometimes catastrophes? If laughter is such a positive, healthy experience, why does it seem to require negativity to fuel it?

If we return to one of the primitive myths, suggested by Rapp (1951), that the first laughter occurred when a caveman hit another man over the head and stole his girlfriend only to exclaim, "Ha, ha—take that!" we can see that aggressive humor requires negativity. In this case, the negativity is bestowed upon the other, allowing the subject to proclaim his superiority with glee in his eye and a chuckle from his mouth. Again, this is a very primitive form of humor—which is quite limited when compared with the level of humor involved in *Seinfeld* or *Curb Your Enthusiasm*. There we find situational humor in which unfortunate twists and turns occur to the protagonists, many of which are caused by their own doing.

But there is something useful in the primitive myth for our purposes, still. The negative is always present in humor because humor is a perception of the negative. It feasts on the negative. Humor, in fact, is one possible human reaction to the negative. In our most primitive example, though, it is the victor who revels in knocking his rival down and taking something of value to him. They laugh as a kind of "icing on the cake"—but they laugh because they are victorious over the other person. Of course, in most cases, the negative must be limited to small doses. If the rival caveman is killed by a crushing blow, it may not be funny, but if he is simply temporarily disabled, that may allow for humor—just as in the Charlie Chaplin movies, nobody is ever seriously injured or killed.

How, though, is the negative transcended in the caveman example? The perpetrator of violence here is faced with a negative situation at the outset. The other person has the goods—the woman, of course. The caveman needs to find a way to overcome this and does so using the most primitive method—physical violence. What is the caveman, then, laughing at? He laughs at the moment of transcendence; the negative situation was not ultimate. His ability to overcome the other and to render the other disabled and helpless is precisely what is funny. It appeared as if the other had the advantage, but that is no longer the case.

Brewster's Millions (Hill, 1985), is a movie in which Richard Pryor brilliantly plays the role of a man whose uncle is extremely wealthy. The uncle challenges Brewster to spend a tremendous amount of money in order to prove himself worthy of inheriting a much larger sum of money. . This, of course, is humorous in itself, but he encounters all kinds of obstacles and even failure as he attempts to spend the money.

Ordinarily, we are all focused on avoiding large expenditures and are engaged in trying to stretch and increase our resources as much as possible. Pryor's character hires workers at ridiculously high salaries, invests in hopeless stocks, and bets on horses that have never won—but each one turns out to *generate* income rather than deplete it. The workers refuse to take the high-salaried job, the stocks go up in value, and the longshot horses, surprisingly, win! Why is this so funny?

Generally, we attempt to save as much as possible and spend prudently. Spending seems easy and the assumption we live with is that, if we were allowed to spend freely, the negative would cease to exist. It is a common assumption that endless resources would provide happiness. But Brewster finds that, even when he has millions to spend and is simply asked to make bad investments, he cannot succeed in this task, either. You cannot win; even when you're trying to lose, you cannot win at that. The negative finds ever new manifestations, ever more clever representations. Here we laugh at the fact that the negative seems inescapable.

Negative situations dominate *Curb Your Enthusiasm* as Larry David attempts to simply live an uncluttered, uncontaminated life, but others seem to always get in the way. They provide the impetus for controversial encounters in which David is forced to act in a painful way. The show is painful, in many ways, because the audience often feels that David would often be better off simply "letting the situation go" but he, instead, feels compelled to challenge the other, which generally leads to more conflict and further difficulties. In one such situation, Larry is waiting in line at a gourmet ice cream store:

> The woman in front of him is requesting sample after sample before deciding which flavor to order. She seems to be in no rush at all and the decision making process is taking forever, while the line gets longer and longer. Our protagonist, Larry, simply cannot take it any longer and, despite the awkwardness, feels compelled to confront the woman, claiming she is a sample-abuser. The encounter goes very poorly as she defends herself from his criticism and he makes his claim even stronger. The scene ends in quite a squabble. Later, it turns out that the woman is a school

board administrator who is in charge of admissions—at a time when Larry's adopted child is seeking admission to this school. He is forced to apologize to her, despite the fact that his claim against the woman (for sampling abuse) was perfectly justified. (Gibbons et al., 1999–2021)

The situation is uncomfortable, difficult, awkward, and painful— from the standpoint of the audience. In fact, many people have told me that they dislike the show *Curb Your Enthusiam* because it's more pain than comedy. What they don't seem to *get* is that the comedy comes from the pain. How does the pain produce humor, though?

Once again, we must remember some of the commonalities involved in humor; for example, the pain or negative cannot be overwhelmingly strong. There's nothing funny about an innocent man being killed because he refused to give up his Nike shoes. If he was slightly harmed, however, there might be some humor there. The stakes, then, must be limited to injury, discomfort, and inconvenience rather than true calamity.

Humor also requires the needed *distance* that the receiver is afforded. Larry is inconvenienced by not getting his ice cream in a timely manner, and, later, his child (actually, it's the child of the woman he is involved with) is denied access to the school that they are hoping for admission to. It is his pain, not ours. But we must feel enough of the pain—but not too much—to appreciate the humor in the situation. Distance and minimization of the negative are, then, preconditions of this form of humor.

But we have, thus far, not addressed the central question: How does "the negative" fuel comedy? What is it about the worst-case scenario that is so funny? A personal example from my family may help to clarify.

My dad collected "punches" on a punch card for the local car wash. He was a man who did not "need" a freebie but relished it with great spirit. Ten washes, ten punches would lead to a free car wash. After the tenth one, he was delighted that he could get his car washed for free. He arrived at the car wash only to find the dreaded, "Closed: Out of business" sign.

This is funny. But notice that it would not be funny if he had only amassed eight punches on his card when the car wash went out of business. Only when the "worst possible" situation occurs can we find it truly humorous. Again, we can see that a free car wash is not a life-or-death situation, and my father's interest in the freebie when it isn't necessary adds some spice to the comedic aspect of this situation. But why is it necessary to have the worst situation represented for humor to emerge?

We can, perhaps, find some of our answer in the popularity of Murphy's Law (2021) in our present culture. The basic principle here is that "If something can go wrong, it will." A mild chuckle usually accompanies the recognition of a case of Murphy's Law. Actually, there are a series of axioms that are now associated with Edward A. Murphy, who was an aerospace engineer who worked on safety-critical systems in the 1940s .

Murphy's Original Law: If there are two or more ways to do something, and one of those ways can result in a catastrophe, then someone will do it.

Murphy's Law: If anything can go wrong, it will.

Murphy's First Corollary: Left to themselves, things tend to go from bad to worse.

Murphy's Second Corollary: It is impossible to make anything foolproof because fools are so ingenious.

Quantized Revision of Murphy's Law: Everything goes wrong all at once.

Murphy's Constant: Matter will be damaged in direct proportion to its value. (Murphy's Laws Site, 2021)

Why is Murphy's Law so humorous? Let's deconstruct this a bit. The "law" states something that, itself, is absurd from the standpoint of common sense and reason. Probabilities would dictate that sometimes the worst outcomes occur and sometimes they do not. In fact, the concept involves a logical contradiction since—if a "bad outcome" occurred every time it could, we would not even be able to recognize a good outcome (nor a bad one, actually). As a declaration, then, it is logically absurd and senseless. But, phenomenologically, it often "seems as if" *anything that can go wrong, does.* You plan an important outdoor event for the middle of July—and, of course, it rains cats and dogs. You are late for work for the first time in two years and your boss just happens to be there to see you enter the office. You plan a surprise for your wife for after work and have everyone ready when she decides, on a whim, to stay at the office for several hours to complete a project.

One aspect that is funny is that we *know* that the law cannot possibly hold any validity. We're somehow, simultaneously, aware of its ridiculousness and believe in its validity or in its power. It is also a way for us to "understand" negative outcomes that seem to come so often and so mercilessly. If there is such a law of the universe, then we were doomed from the start. We can "laugh it off" or "chalk it up" to Murphy's Law. This also relieves us of any responsibility (and therefore guilt) for the unfortunate outcome.

That simultaneous perception of the absurdity of the "law," along with the formality of calling it an axiom or a law, presents the kind of incongruity that humor thrives on. We laugh at the absurdity that perhaps there is a kind of "brutal justice" that is interfering in the natural world, causing everything that can go wrong to, in fact, go wrong.

Whether it's a missing report, a set of keys, or a sweater, you can expect to find it right after you replace it.

Have you noticed that the most valuable items are irretrievably damaged, while things you don't care about last forever?

When you try to force things to work in your favor, they are apt to get worse. If you're parenting a teenager, you have already worked this out. The more pressure you apply, the less likely you are to be successful.

When spending the day waiting for an oil delivery or repairman, they will only arrive after you have climbed into the shower.

If you are not looking for a certain tool (pliers for example), they are always there, and you know exactly where they are. Once you finally need the tool, you can't find it. (Khurana, 2019)

In a later chapter on irony, we will see that some of these cases of Murphy's Law include at least a "soft" form of irony. In each case, however, what these situations have in common are that, despite the best considerations and planning, life throws a curveball at us in the form of a negative outcome. Even if one adopts the most positive of attitudes toward these outcomes, we can, at best, shrug our shoulders and laugh it off. Note, however, that none of these examples involve anything life-threatening or catastrophic, allowing for the possibility of a comedic perspective.

There is a tendency toward neuroticism as a component of the appreciation of negative humor. In fact, some theorists have suggested that the essence of neuroticism is precisely the use of the negative in order to protect themselves. What could they be protecting themselves against in their focus on the negative? The neurotic who focuses on what is wrong with their life constantly protects themselves against true failure. If one is focused on the attempt to satisfy the project to be, then failure is a possibility. If one views oneself as subject to all sorts of negativity, then failure is to be expected and not a fault of the person.

> I interviewed for a position today. The waiting room was filled with people who were really poised and attractive. It was like being in *The Stepford Wives*, with all these plastic-looking, beautiful women. When they finally asked me to come in for the interview, I tripped and fell flat on my face. It was hilarious. As if I even had a chance to begin with. Well, I won't be hearing from them; that's for sure! (fictional vignette)

This woman, clearly, is using the negative as a way of protecting herself from the possibility of self-based failure. She focuses on the attractiveness but also on the shallowness of the other contenders to demonstrate that she doesn't have a chance of succeeding to begin with. The comedic event of tripping on the way in provides comic relief for the story but also allows her to attribute the failure of her interview to circumstances beyond her control. The belief that she was "doomed from the start" is evident in her description.

But the appreciation of "negative humor" can also be based on a much deeper level of insight. When the negative appears, therefore, one can appreciate the humor precisely because it is unavoidable, in an ultimate sense. If a person wallows in the notions involved in Murphy's Law, they are probably engaging in a neurotic, self-as-victim mode of being. But if one recognizes the inevitability of the negative, this can give rise to a profound appreciation for humor that focuses on the way in which the negative appears—perhaps when it is least expected or when one is least prepared for it.

PART III

FINAL FORMS OF HUMOR EXAMINED

Chapter 11

INCONGRUITY AND DISCREPANCY HUMOR

I n this return to forms of humor, let's now consider a domain of humor that has received a great deal of attention in the literature. Many theorists have talked about the role of incongruity in humor (Hull, et al., 2017; Morreall, 1987). This theory states simply that, when two things that are incongruous, surprising, or unrelated are placed side by side, we find it humorous.

> I don't know if there is an afterlife, but I'm taking along a couple of pairs of underwear just in case. (Allen, 2021)

The Woody Allen one-liner is a classic case of incongruity. The setup is concern about something very philosophical and broad, which requires deep thought: Is there an afterlife? There are two possibilities implied: Either there is an afterlife—in which case one would, naturally, be concerned with correct conduct, possibly living one's life in harmony with God or whatever religious stance is adopted—or there is not. In that case, one might be faced with a kind of existential "situation" of meaninglessness or despair, or a kind of radical freedom. The concrete specificity of "bringing along underwear" comes, therefore, as a surprise.

It is not, however, the surprise itself that constitutes humor here—though it may be a precondition of this form of incongruous humor. If Allen had said, "I'm taking along a couple of nice shirts just in case," it may have been funny but not as funny as "underwear." Why not? It is because underwear is even more discrepant from philosophical reflection than shirts are. Underwear is private and attends to the physical creatureness of the person, which is as discrepant as possible from the metaphysical. Also, underwear is petty—and not necessary—but something we cling to in "earthly existence" as a kind of artificial form of privacy. In fact, underwear itself lends itself to humor quite well. "I looked in and saw my professor in nothing but his undies!" Underwear is something we all share but represents that private reality that we pretend does not exist. It's clothing but not really clothing. It covers but also reveals. It's the perfect object for humor to play with, which is why there is so much humor focused on underwear.

> Time flies, though, huh? But I feel young. And do you know how I stay feeling young, ladies and gentlemen? I'll share my secret with you: I live in a senior citizen retirement community.
>
> Women in the workplace—we still have big strides to make. Girlfriend of mine just got a new job. First question the new boss asked her was if she could make a good cup of coffee . . . yeah, she stormed right out of that Starbucks. (Leifer, in AZ Quotes, 2021)

Carol Leifer is a master of incongruity. She begins each of these vignettes with a serious topic—fear of getting old or women's rights in the workplace—and surprises the audience with an unexpected twist. The first part "draws the audience in" to being concerned about the serious situation; the punchline provides a "pop out" of the serious situation, allowing us to be relieved of that concern.

> I love being married. It's so great to find that one special person you want to annoy for the rest of your life.

My grandmother was a very tough woman. She buried three husbands and two of them were just napping.

My husband and I are either going to buy a dog or have a child. We can't decide whether to ruin our carpets or ruin our lives. (Rudner, in AZ Quotes, 2021)

Rita Rudner's classic comments about family and marriage have, as their punchline, the blatant truth about how we may, at base, feel about those with whom we're closest. She plays with the contrast between the standard view of family as those we love and respect and the darker truth about the realities of family life. In each case, the first line is a simple, socially acceptable statement about her family, but the second states the blunter truth.

Groucho Marx, about his experience on an African safari: "One morning, I shot an elephant in my pajamas. How he got in my pajamas, I'll never know." (Marx, in AZ Quotes, 2021)

The incongruity here lies in the change in image that is inspired by the surprise twist in the story. As we read the first part, it is perfectly clear that he means he was wearing pajamas while he shot an elephant, assumed to be in the distance (or at least a few feet away!). The phrase "in my pajamas" is allowed, in the second part, to be literal. Now we are forced to consider an elephant that is actually in Groucho's pajamas—a very different situation altogether and one that is humorous in itself. But the brilliance of this story is, of course, in the switch—and the fact that we cannot deny that the second articulation is, in fact, literal and correct, grammatically and semantically. The following joke was adapted from Cohen (1999)

Early one morning a man awoke in a state of terrible anxiety because of the dream he had been having. He immediately called his psychiatrist, and—after making a special plea because of his distress he was granted an appointment that morning even though it was not the day for seeing his psychiatrist. When he arrived in the doctor's office, he said, "I had the most awful dream you can imagine. In it I cursed out my father, left my job and family, and wound up homeless on the streets. I woke up shaking and sweating, and I called you immediately. Then I had a quick piece of toast and some coffee and ran down here to see you."

The psychiatrist stroked his beard, thought for a moment, and then said, "You call that a decent breakfast?"

This joke seems to meet with a variety of responses. The incongruity, of course, lies in the difference between our expectations of the psychiatrist's response and his actual one. We expect that a psychiatrist would be deeply interested in the content of the patient's reported dream, but, instead, he focuses on a much more trivial matter that seems relatively inconsequential. Some researchers have focused on the *surprise factor* in incongruity humor as the central factor. We are surprised by the emphasis placed on the trivial by the psychiatrist. Is that what is humorous, though? Let's examine another joke before determining the formula involved in incongruity humor.

I hate when women compare men to dogs. Men are not dogs. Dogs are loyal. I've never found any strange panties in my dog's house. (Sykes, as quoted in Scott, 2018)

Clearly, it is not simply a matter of surprise—and that is one of the weaknesses of the "incongruity theory" of humor. It is not simply surprise that makes something funny. There must be other elements involved as well. For example, here the psychiatrist being unconcerned with the "psychological" and, instead, concerned with something trivial and physical is a large part of the humor. That we didn't see it coming adds to the humor or may even be integral to the humor here, but it is more than that. What we see here is quite familiar at this point in this discussion of humor. The presumed expert turns out to be a goon; even when the most obvious case of what he purports to be the truth is presented to him, he does not recognize it or dismisses it. He's a false authority, which, of course, is one of the most prominent sources of humor.

> The secret of staying young is to live honestly, eat slowly, and lie about your age. (Ball, 2021)

> In every group of girlfriends, there's like one who is the sluttiest. And if you don't have that friend—you're that friend! Let's be real. (Schumer, 2017)

> With kids it's so funny because they're not strong enough to kill you. But they want to kill you so bad! (Fey, 2017)

All of these jokes begin with a statement that is sensible and agreeable—but end with a zinger. The zinger is something that has the ring of truth—you need to lie about your age to really "stay young," or you may be that sluttiest of your friends—but is unexpected, given the beginning proposition. That punchline, moreover, provides a potential dose of reality that may not be appreciated except within a comedic mode.

Another common form of humor is the juxtaposition of the *most important* with the trivial.

> What do Alexander the Great and Winnie the Pooh have in common?

> They have the same middle name. (unknown origin)

Here the receiver is thinking about essential elements that would be important comparisons, despite the obvious differences between these two entities. The response that they both have the same middle name—"the"—is a surprising twist. First, "the" is really not a middle name, so it must come as a surprise to hear that this is the commonality between them. Also, there is probably no other word in the English language that is more devoid of content than "the." The triviality of this commonality is the surprising incongruity that provides humor.

> The 2000 year old man (Brooks & Reiner, 1960/2009) has been in a state of slumber for a long, long time. He awakens from that slumber and is going to be interviewed by Carl Reiner. There is no doubt that he must have the most profound wisdom of any man alive, having the greatest perspective on life possible. As he awakens, his first words are, "Do I have a taste in my mouth!"

Again, the expectation of wisdom and profundity from a man who has lived longer than anyone ever has is incongruous with the triviality (but reality) of having a bad taste in one's mouth after resting for so long. The buildup, which emphasizes the expected depth of insight that a 2,000-year-old man would have, led to a more powerful juxtaposition of incongruity between profound and trivial. Often, the trivial in humor is tied to the bodily. In fact, comedy utilizes bodily aspects probably as much as biology does—farts, shit, urine, body odor, physical aggression, bodily injury, attractiveness or ugliness, etc. Very often, though, this contrast between "the bodily" and the "mind, soul, or self" is utilized in just this fashion. Comedy could even be said to have a basic metaphysics that says that the mind, soul, and self are wonderful constructions, but the bottom line (concrete truth) is the body.

> Sarah: "I went through a terrible depression and I remember my stepfather saying, 'What does it feel like?'"

Jerry: "Excuse me, waiter, do you have any half and half?" (To Sarah) "I'm so sorry."

Sarah: "I just said, I went through a terrible depression as a kid and you ask for half and half?"

Jerry: "In the comedian's view of life, those things are kind of equal." (Seinfeld, 2013)

This is part of a conversation that took place between Sarah Silverman and Jerry Seinfeld at a coffee shop in Seinfeld's wonderful *Comedians in Cars Getting Coffee* series. Just as Sarah opens up and reveals a very deep and personal aspect of herself, Jerry interrupts to ask the waiter for half and half. Even more disturbing, but also funny, is the fact that there is milk at the table already—so that the request is purely a matter of preference and a very trivial one at that. Seinfeld's remark that these two very disparate elements of life to a comedian are kind of equal is very telling. Humor certainly utilizes that sort of contrast consistently. The contrast between deep, personal matters and trivial, personal preferences is often the focus of humor.

In *Annie Hall*, Woody Allen and his girlfriend are at a very sophisticated party with high society people who are seemingly all talking politics or world affairs. They dip into a private room and Woody makes an impassioned plea for them to have sex right there. He says, "This will be great. They're all talking societal stuff out there in the cocktail party and we'll be in here, quietly humping!" (Allen, 1977)

Again, the contrast between society talk and the physical (sexuality) is what drives the humor. But it is not simply the incongruity involved in the contrast between the intellectual and the physical that is at stake here. Allen's humorous moment is in the assertion of the *reality* of the physical over and above that of the intellectual. He portrays the intellectual conversation of high society people as shallow and phony. They are not really sincere but engage in this type of small talk, primarily to "fit in" socially. This "society-talk" is then contrasted with the pure physicality of sexuality—which has the undeniable advantage.

An elderly woman announces to her friends that she is getting married again.

"Is he handsome?" one asks.

"No," the woman says.

"Is he smart?" another asks.

"No," the woman replies.

"Well is he rich?" the third one asks.

"No," she says again.

"Then why are you marrying him?" they blurt out at once.

"He drives at night!" (Rogoff, 2014)

Once again, we see a case of the more lofty, noble traits being laid side by side with a more basic, primitive need for night transportation. The humor in this joke lies with the recognition of the importance of the physical, primary needs over the more acceptable and expected characteristics that one might look for in a dating partner.

Deadpan Humor as Incongruity

In our earlier discussion of deadpan humor, we saw a similar incongruity construction. The humorist here delivers his lines in a purely unemotional manner. The material, however, is "wild and crazy" and contrasts sharply with the emotionless delivery. But is there a similarly biased incongruity here? Is it the emotionless delivery that reveals the critical reality, or is the *content* of the spoken material that which is real?

> I bought some powdered water, but I didn't know what to add to it.

> I was born by Caesarean section, but you really can't tell . . . except that when I leave my house, I always go out the window. (Wright, 2021)

Steven Wright's one liners are outrageous. They challenge our conceptions of reality and would probably be funny regardless of the delivery. The deadpan style in which he delivers his lines, however, adds another contrast or incongruity—between the simple, unemotional and the *reality-challenging* conceptions. The audience member is almost forced to ask the obvious question, "How can you be so unemotional when all this bizarre stuff is going on?" In fact, the desired effect on the audience is that they are both laughing and incredulous—or incredulous and laughing, in that order. The "way out" is contrasted as incongruous with the "matter of fact," which, in contrast, seems out of place.

Here, though, it seems that deadpan survives on the sheer power of the incongruity. The receiver is placed directly at the center of the two extremes. One is surprised by the lack of emotion exhibited by the deadpan comic and also by the extent to which the spoken material is "out of the bounds of reality." Both are preposterous! In fact, the preposterousness of the situation is precisely why it is funny. Both the complete lack of emotion and the way-out material beg of reality; neither can be valid. The receiver, then, is allowed to traverse beyond both into laughter if they are so inclined. Once again, transcendence is at the core of the humor because the receiver is, at first, caught between two realities, both of which must be rejected, and then, through humor, is able to extricate themself from the untenable nature of the conflict they are in.

What is this extrication, though? Where does the receiver of deadpan go, mentally? Keep in mind that deadpan seems to be the type of humor that must be repeated. It thrives on the one-liner and on repeated instances of itself. When Wright delivers one-liner after one-liner, the effect is additive or maybe even exponential. In other words, it isn't just the momentary experience of the joke that the audience member is receiving; the effect that is created by repeated measures is that of a *state of mind*. The state of mind comes about through a process that has—at its core—humor as the end result.

In the case of deadpan, the two extremes are manifest by the comic. The receiver, then, is either faced with the most negative of all circumstances—a choice of two realities, side by side, that are both too extreme and delivered by the same mind. He or she is forced to try to reconcile these opposites, which is not really possible. At the last minute, though, humor erupts as the irreconcilable nature of the two is recognized and, therefore, transcended. This "popping out," though, is not permanent. On the contrary, it's quite transient and ephemeral because, even though one can take delight in the absurdity of these two choices, especially as they are proposed by the same source, one cannot truly transcend by humor—especially this type of humor. It's quite brief, which is why a chuckle is a common response to deadpan humor, not a belly laugh. However, this often is an entry point to greater laughter, which is why comedians like Steven Wright and Mitch Hedberg utilized a quick barrage of one-liners, which led to riotous eruptions from their audiences.

Absurdist Humor

One subset of incongruity and discrepancy humor is what can be labeled as absurdist humor. This form of humor is also based on an unexpected twist that takes the receiver by surprise. In this case, however, the claims that the jokes make are not only unpredictable but also unintelligible.

> What was strange was that Old Nahamcan was younger than Young Nahamcan. (Allen, 1973)

> I used the wrong key to open the door to my house. So I started up the house and was driving down the street and I found myself yelling, "Get off of my property!" to other drivers. (Wright, 2021)

It is simply not possible that the father of a child can be younger than his son. Yet the claim here is that this is precisely the case, and Woody Allen insists that it is true and that it is a mystery that is unexplainable. Absurdist humor plays on the impossible in the most blatant and manifest manner. In the case of using the wrong key (presumably, the car keys) and "starting up the house," again, the description of events is simply absurd. One cannot "start up a house and drive down the street" as if it were a car by using the wrong key.

Yet absurdist humor does tap into fantasy by pushing reality to its extremes. It is so ridiculous that it forces one to suspend reality and imagine a reality that is not subject to ordinary spatial/temporal bounds. Literature, of course, has a long history of such absurdity.

> As Gregor Samsa awoke one morning from uneasy dreams, he found himself transformed in his bed into a gigantic insect. (Kafka & Bernofsky, 1981)

Kafka's famous *The Metamorphosis* rests entirely on this absurd transformation that, once allowed by the reader, allows for a viewpoint and a commentary that flows from that acceptance. But, interestingly, it is hardly funny, perhaps because the absurd transformation that has occurred is horrifying and demeaning, to the point where it is hard to maintain a humorous perspective on the situation. Successful absurdist humor, on the other hand, must be harmless and silly.

> I came home one night and found that my house had been broken into. Everything had been stolen and replaced with exact replicas. (Wright, 2021)

This joke is interesting because it is *possible* that the event in question did, in fact, occur. It is, however, both unlikely to have occurred and also unlikely to be detected if the furniture and everything else in the house were exact replicas. This dual reality—that an event of that sort could occur and that one would not be likely to recognize it—adds to the humor. Why would that happen? It is much more likely that the reporter of this event is paranoid, psychotic, or just "having a bad day" than that his statement is accurate. But the fact that no real consequence would occur in such a situation allows us to find the absurdity funny.

Having mistakenly time-traveled to another civilization, a character in a book called *The Time Machine* (Swatzwelder, 2004) encountered the following absurd situation:

> I was also curious, and growing increasingly so, to know where a guy could get something to eat around here. I tried buying something at a restaurant, but they only took "credits," whatever those were. I held out some dollar bills, but they said those weren't credits. I held up a button. That wasn't a credit. I shook my fist at them. No credits there either. Eventually I found out a "credit" was a screwdriver. I checked my pockets, but I didn't have any "credits" on me. I went to a hardware store and they had a screwdriver, all right, but they wanted a shitload of screwdrivers for it. (Swartzwelder, 2004, p. 117)

From the inside of this predicament, it would undoubtedly be torturous, but from the outside, we might find this exceedingly funny. Of course, the absurdity here is an old conundrum; you need X, but in order to obtain X, you are required to have X. Furthermore, the use of screwdrivers as a monetary unit is, itself, rather capricious, odd, and, yes, absurd. Notice that much of the rest of the story, though, holds reality steady. You do go to a hardware store to obtain screwdrivers—just as we do in our current world—except that you need them to obtain them. This is somewhat akin to going to the bank to get money but you need money to get the money you need.

> A mother and daughter are having a nice lunch in a fancy restaurant. At one point, the daughter intends to simply say, "Please pass the salt," but instead says, "You have ruined my whole life!" (unknown source)

If we were to psychoanalyze this joke, of course, we'd easily conclude that the daughter has some deep, underlying anger and resentment toward her mother. For the moment, though, we can just appreciate the absurdity of the mistake in speech. There's a lot of distance between "pass the salt" and "you have ruined my whole life" that is hard to explain. It's patently absurd that you can go from one to the other.

The humor in absurdity allows us to see the bounds of spatial/ temporal, linear reality and to appreciate the freedom from the limits of that reality. In the highest quality of absurdist humor, there are elements of reality present, as in the examples just seen— where, in fact, screwdrivers are sold at a hardware store. But reality is stretched or challenged by another element that, literally, makes no sense and presents an impossible predicament that cannot be handled or overcome by logic and reason.

People Who Thrive on Incongruity and Discrepancy Humor

Some folks love to be surprised and are perhaps more tolerant of the conflicts this form of humor presents. If one finds everyday, mundane life to be boring and predictable, one way of coping with that boredom would be this form of surprising and conflicting humor. Those who employ incongruity and discrepancy humor, moreover, delight in "surprising the other" who is viewed as naive and the unexpected "victim" of the twist utilized in this form of humor. What is perhaps most appreciated by the lover of this type of humor is the cleverness of recognizing those unexpected twists. One note about incongruity humor in terms of hierarchy is in order: It is not at all clear that all incongruity humor would be considered a high-level or highbrow form of humor. For example, the examples in this chapter of absurdist humor can be quite silly and perhaps would not require a great deal of wisdom or sophistication to appreciate them.

Chapter 12

IRONIC HUMOR

Irony is often considered the most advanced form of humor. Indeed, studies reveal that children simply cannot comprehend irony until somewhere between 5 and 8 years old (Angeleri et al., 2014). Irony, moreover, is generally considered the highest type of humor. What makes irony so revered? What are the conditions under which irony takes place, and what does it mean if one appreciates ironic humor?

First, one must recognize that ironic humor is not the sort of humor that provides a big belly laugh or a fall-on-the-floor-cracking-up kind of laughter. Irony relies on a more sophisticated perception on the part of the perceiver, often built on a somewhat complex narrative that takes place over a length of time. Let's start with some examples of what has been called irony and see if we can move toward some useful definitions and distinctions within ironic situations.

Though she hated her father and repudiated all that he stood for, even estranging herself from him, her own chosen husband had many of the characteristics of her dad. She couldn't believe that she—who detested him so completely—married a man who is very similar to her father!

A man brings his car into the collision repair center after a minor accident. While in the shop, during a test-drive by the mechanic, the car is in another accident that totals the car.

A child runs away from his friend who is trying to throw a water balloon at him—and, in his effort to get away, falls into the pool.

A post on Facebook argues about the uselessness of social media in communicating anything important.

A fire station burns down. (Kittelstad, 2021)

Many of these examples may strike the reader as not particularly funny. Some of these situations might even appear, most immediately, as "hypocrisy," rather than ironic humor. For example, the Facebook poster who argues the dangers and uselessness of Facebook while posting their remarks on that very same social media site could be indicted for hypocrisy. Other examples may be regarded as, simply, cases of "bad luck," such as the situation where the automobile owner attempts to get his car repaired and winds up with a more damaged car as a result. Indeed, irony has been one of the most difficult concepts to define and explain, resulting in a good deal of controversy about the meaning and definition of the term itself.

One of the examples of this controversy erupted in literature circles around the Alanis Morissette (1996) song "Ironic." Some argued that there is virtually no irony at all in the song, while others defended the song as containing several examples of irony.

A closer analysis reveals a manifold of types of situations described in this song. In some cases—like the "black fly in your Chardonnay"—one can easily argue that no irony is present but that this is simply a matter of *bad luck* or even just inconvenience. On the other hand, a "death row pardon two minutes too late" seems to contain a touch of irony, though certainly not much in the way of humor. Rain on one's wedding day, again, appears as an unfortunate outcome. Perhaps if one chose a date during the least rainy season precisely for that reason, some irony might be detected there. From the little analysis given here, we can see why this song led to so much contention among the literary critics.

Let's take a broader look at the proposed types of irony and their definitions. The traditional typology for forms of irony proposes three, and sometimes four, types: verbal irony, situational irony, dramatic irony, and (sometimes) Socratic irony. Of course, for purposes of this study of humor, this typology might be somewhat revised. Socratic irony, for example, does not seem to yield a particularly comedic reaction. Some forms of situational and even verbal irony, moreover, may also not be considered humorous.

Verbal Irony

Verbal irony is defined by "the use of words to express something other than and especially the opposite of the literal meaning" (*Merriam-Webster*, 2021). A great deal of effort has been allotted to the attempt to distinguish verbal irony from sarcasm. In fact, that distinction is not sustainable, as there is quite a bit of overlap between the two. The difference, presumably, lies in the *intent* involved in the articulation. Verbal irony occurs when people say one thing but mean another. Sarcasm, however, connotes a little bit of a mean twist or a derogatory statement. Sarcasm, then, would contain more of a "biting" intent. The difference, then, is said to be a quantitative, but not a qualitative one. Here are some classic examples of verbal irony:

> That is as clear as mud.
>
> I guess it's my lucky day (after two car accidents in one day)!
>
> Gentlemen, you can't fight in here; this is the war room! (Kubrick, *Dr. Strangelove*)
>
> After a terrible blind date, a woman calls her friend and says, "He was as friendly as a rattlesnake."
>
> A boyfriend plans to propose to his girlfriend on the night she

cancels on him to stay home and binge-watch *Grey's Anatomy*. He replies, "Sure. It's not like I had anything special planned." (Gunner, 2021a)

Can you distinguish between verbal irony and sarcasm here? One could imagine this list being utilized as examples for either one. What is at play in verbal irony, though? A remark is made that carries a deeper meaning than simply a straightforward comment. The speaker is conveying that the situation does not meet a set of reasonable standards. They do so by demonstrating a number of things in the process: 1) they know what those standards are, 2) the material or situation does not meet those standards, and 3) they see humor in the situation. Wherein lies the humor, though? One factor is the "reasonableness" of the request or the demand here. That the situation doesn't even approximate the most reasonable expectations suggests absurdity, which is pointed out by the sarcastic or verbal-ironic comment.

In the last example given here, of the boyfriend who planned this monumental occasion in which to propose, his remark is, on the surface, straightforward. The intention, however, to the informed audience, is to underscore the discrepancy between simply relinquishing a plan because it is not convenient and being forced to retreat when the project was of enormous importance. Perhaps here we could say that there is verbal irony in the fact that the girlfriend is rejecting seeing him in order to watch TV when he is planning a monumental proposal—and there is sarcasm in his verbal statement that, "It's not like I had anything special planned."

Dramatic Irony

In a suspenseful film, the character goes into a house they think is empty, but the audience knows that the killer is in the house. In Shakespeare's *Hamlet*, we are aware that Hamlet knows the truth about his father's murder and that Hamlet is not mad. He is simply deceiving others so that he can plan his revenge.

In the *Star Wars* movies, Luke does not know Darth Vader is his father until Episode V, but the audience knows sooner.

In the TV show *Smallville*, Clark Kent comments that in the future he does not want to put on a suit and fly around, but the audience knows he will.

In the movie *Toy Story*, Buzz Lightyear thinks he is a real space ranger, but the other toys and the audience know that he is just a toy.

Hank Schrader in *Breaking Bad* is a DEA agent looking for crystal-meth producer "Heisenberg." We know that "Heisenberg" is Schrader's brother-in-law, Walter White, while Hank has no idea. (Gunner, 2021b)

In dramatic irony, the audience is made aware of an important element of the story while the characters in the drama are unaware of the "secret." The complexity and discrepancy in the narrative, for the audience versus the characters, allows dramatic irony to be considered under the heading of irony, but most of the examples do not provide a great deal of humor. When humor does appear here, it is usually in the form of seeing the character as "inside of" an illusion and therefore acting from a tunnel-vision standpoint, relative to what "we know" of the situation. The character, then, can be seen as "understandably foolish," but foolish nevertheless.

The irony, in dramatic irony, then, is all *contained within the unknowing character.* She thinks he's a safe person to be alone with— when it turns out (and the audience knows) that he's the killer that everyone is searching for. Moreover, she has exactly the profile of the type of victim he seeks out. Is this funny? Not at all. But it is ironic in the sense that the truth is not what one could reasonably suspect. Of course, a great deal depends on the outcome. If the poor maiden is assaulted or even killed, there is no humor whatsoever, despite the audience/character discrepancy. If the woman succeeds in extricating herself from the situation unscathed, perhaps we can laugh at her innocence and at our unique position of knowing while she was unaware. At any rate, the humor value of dramatic irony is limited and, therefore, not worthy of further discussion here.

Situational Irony

> A marriage counselor files for divorce.
>
> The police station is robbed.
>
> A Wall Street Investor is constantly making fun of clients who are not willing to make a risky investment; the investor himself loses everything in the stock market.
>
> A wife hears of her husband's death and begins to imagine a life of freedom from the tyranny of the marriage. The husband, however, is not dead and shows up at the house. She is so shocked that she suffers a fatal heart attack upon his arrival at home. (Kittelstad, 2021)

In situational irony, there is, again, an unexpected result, given the previous conditions. Marriage counselors would, at a naive level, be expected to have good marriages. Police stations should be free from crime since it is their mission to prevent crime. The surprise in situational irony is in direct relation to the original conditions or nature of reality that is articulated in the situation.

Notice, however, that our definition of situational irony is intentionally broad enough to cover a great deal of ground. In fact, it is probably too broad because unexpected results are fairly common and there may not be any irony involved. Once in a while, the newspaper is not delivered to my front door. This event is never expected, but it's also not ironic. Irony would only appear if there is some *significance* to the newspaper's disappearance this morning. Perhaps I was waiting all week for Thursday's *Times*, when my editorial was to be published—and, ironically enough, that is the one day this year that the paper was not delivered. Otherwise, as we saw with many examples in the Morrisette song, it's simply a matter of bad luck or happenstance. Shit happens. It's not irony unless there is some *connection* between the bad event and previous circumstances that appears to be more than chance.

> We spend the first twelve months of our children's lives teaching them to walk and talk and the next twelve telling them to sit down and shut up. (Diller, in AZ Quotes, 2021)

In some cases, there is a kind of personal justice or karma that is implied by the ironic situation. Situational irony appears when a person is hypocritical in their actions. A politician who, for example, claims (in all public messages) to support the farmers while simultaneously voting against all bills that would provide aid to the farmers is, ironically, hurting those he claims to support. The irony becomes even greater when his hypocritical stance leads to a disadvantage for himself. For example, he may fail to be reelected as a result of his track record. Notice, however, that this type of ironic outcome would be funny, perhaps, but only to that politician's opposition. They may get a hearty laugh out of his election loss. His supporters, however, would likely not view this outcome as humorous. Irony is not always humorous. When this kind of self-induced karmic turn of events occurs in a meaningful manner—justice enters the picture—and situational irony begins to become what we will call deep irony.

Deep Irony

> A husband and wife who loved to play golf were driving home one night and ran into a bridge abutment, and both were killed. They arrived in heaven and found it was a beautiful golf course with a lovely clubhouse and fabulous greens. It was free and only for them, and the husband said, "You want to play a round?"
>
> She said, "Sure." They teed off on the first hole, and she notices that the husband is upset at something. "What's wrong?" she asks.
>
> "You know, if it hadn't been for your stupid oat bran, we could have been here YEARS ago!" (Keillor, 2003, p. 88)

This is a clear case of irony, if there ever was one. What the husband and wife strove for (living a healthy life that would lead to longevity) turned out to *prevent* them from obtaining what they really wanted. It was precisely that which they did to avoid the negative (eat lots of oat bran) that led to their not reaching their goal (beauty, happiness, freedom) as soon as possible. But there is more than common irony in this story. The story illustrates that one can induce their own circumstances by one's own actions. This is *deep irony*—not just happenstance.

Deep irony tells us that what we strive for in a particular domain leads to a set of circumstances that prevent us from reaching that goal. One takes on a new job in order to pay the bills but, in doing so, incurs more expenses (daycare, car expenses, etc.) that nullify the gain involved. By pursuing only incredibly beautiful models for dating partners, one may wind up without any partner at all. It is this *self-induced* form of suffering that is at the core of deep irony.

At first glance, deep irony would seem to be the most crippling and disturbing form of irony, since it implies that our attempts to reach our goals may be futile ones. Whatever action taken will, in fact, *backfire* and lead to the opposite conclusion than the one we are seeking. But deep irony, therefore, leads to a self-reflection about the motives involved in the actions. Should the woman whose husband recently died be gleefully enjoying the freedom this provides? Should the man who tries to move up the ladder by complimenting and manipulating the bosses (leading to an ironic result of him being fired for being insincere) be blindly seeking upward mobility?

One of the reasons that deep irony constitutes humor is that it is, indeed, limited to a particular domain so that the conditions arrived at in the deep ironic situation are not as serious as they might be if the situation was broader. We can laugh at the couple who religiously ate oat bran to avoid death because, even though they could have reached paradise sooner, all is well in the end.

> Gary Kremen, the founder of Match.com, encouraged everyone he knew to join it, including his girlfriend. She eventually left him for a man she met on Match.com. (Newspaper Online, 2016)

Kremen creates a matchmaking company that leads his girlfriend, through his own direction, to finding a better match through his own company! We can laugh at this because relationships, though important, are not critical—especially at the *dating level*.

> A hurricane is approaching and the community is advised to evacuate. One man seems strangely indifferent to the evacuation mandate, however. "God will take care of me. I'll stay in my house, which God provided and which has always kept me comfortable."
>
> The winds are increasing and rains are becoming heavy. One of this man's neighbors pulls up to the man's house in his van and says, "Hey, I've got room in my van. Why don't you grab your

valuables and jump in the car and we can get out of here before it gets really bad?"

The man politely declines, saying, "Don't worry. God will take care of me. You go on and be safe. I can always move up to the second floor of my beautiful house. Thanks for the offer, though."

The water continues to rise, though, and after a couple of hours another neighbor approaches the man's house in a boat and says, "It's getting really bad. Hop in my boat with your valuables and we can get to higher ground and be safe."

The man, again, declines, repeating the same phrase that he continually uses, "God will take care of me. I can always move up to the third floor. Thank you very much for the offer, though."

Finally, the flooding is so prominent in his house that the man is forced to get out on his roof. He's sitting on the roof when a helicopter approaches and the driver yells out to the man, "Let me pick you up. I can get you, safely, on this helicopter and take you to a safe place." Again, the man insists that, "God will take care of me. I don't need any help but thanks for the offer."

The man, finally, drowns in the flood that continues to worsen. He arrives in heaven and is able to approach God with a very challenging question, "God. You must have seen that I was in trouble. Why didn't you save me?"

God looks at the man with incredulity. "What do you mean? I tried to save you several times. I sent a man with a car, a neighbor in a boat, and even a helicopter!" (The Epistle, 2021)

The irony here is potent because the man's core beliefs are consistent with the religious life, yet the outcome, ironically, does not reflect that. His interpretation of those beliefs is, somehow, not conducive to a positive outcome despite those beliefs being rock-solid. What the story tells us is that, even if you have faith and that faith is warranted (there is a God and he is looking out for you), you may misinterpret the manifestation of God's work, leading to your own personal demise. Faith is not enough; one must also be able to correctly interpret the workings of God in the real world in which we live. This constitutes deep irony because it is precisely the man's faith and beliefs that lead him to the worst of all outcomes.

> A woman works so hard, with the goal of finally retiring and enjoying the fruits of her labor. But she winds up incurring a heart attack from overworking and passing away, just before she was planning to retire. (fictional vignette)

> Bill Hillman, a bull running enthusiast, wrote a book called *Fiesta: How to Survive the Bulls of Pamplona,* all about how to avoid being gored by bulls during the "running of the bulls" ceremonies in Spain. Three weeks after the release of the book, he was gored twice in the thigh by a bull. (Ludwig, 2014)

The first of these examples represents a good example of deep irony since it is precisely the effort made (hard work for many years) that leads to the opposite conclusion from the person's intention. She dies before ever being able to retire and enjoy the fruits of her labor. The Bill Hillman example, on the other hand, may not completely satisfy our requirements for deep irony, though there is an undeniable quality of irony involved in the narrative. If he became "overconfident" in his bullfighting techniques or "let his guard down" after perfecting his approach and publishing it, then the example does, indeed, satisfy our criteria for deep irony.

We don't know, however, whether it was simple happenstance that he lost his battle with the bull after recently publishing his book. One way of determining whether a particular example fits our criteria is whether there is a *moral lesson to be learned* from the events involved. If so, then the person has engaged in deep irony; if not, they may have simply been the victim of bad luck, however ironic that particular form of bad luck appears to be. Notice, also, that neither of these examples are particularly humorous, since the consequences in each case are rather severe (death and serious injury).

The lines between deep irony and the next form of humor—wisdom humor—are certainly not clear cut. The distinction between irony and wisdom humor can, in fact, be subtle and difficult to detect. Deep irony, though, tends to be limited to the *certain domain* in which it is contained. The man who seeks upward mobility in an extreme way (thus leading to his getting fired) can learn through deep irony that blind ambition in the workplace does not work and is not moral. The couple in our lead story here can learn that simply seeking a long life is not, in itself, valuable. The quality of life is also important. Faith is not sufficient; one must also be realistic and be able to recognize aspects of reality that may, in fact, manifest God's work. Deep irony informs about the particularities of a domain of life and, one can say, provides both humor and also, potentially, insight. But it is, indeed, limited to a domain of life and not as broad as wisdom, which we will examine in the next chapter.

People Who Enjoy Ironic Humor

As the forms of humor become more and more sophisticated through this loose hierarchical march through them, we can say in a rather sweeping statement that more sophisticated *people* are more likely to revel in something like irony than, for example, physical humor. But that does not prohibit the sophisticated person from enjoying "lower" or more base forms, as well. We all have bodies and much of humor is lowbrow and appreciated by the masses. But those who particularly revel in ironic humor may be the folks who like to delve deeper, beyond the surface, into the more complex and philosophical avenues of life.

There is, as well, a kind of "ironic view" of life that can be identified and described. Those who enjoy ironic humor are ready for or, as psychologists like to say, *primed for* twists and turns that are meaningful and interpretable. Irony is, perhaps, the opposite of random. If one works their whole life with an eye on the joys of retirement, but they work so hard that they prevent themselves from enjoying those fruits, it is not at all a random occurrence. It is "in the cards" that the consequence follows from the behavior that initiates that consequence. The view of life inherent here is one that involves meaning, karma, and even a kind of justice. This meaningful perspective on life, moreover, borders on and represents the beginning of a kind of wisdom—which we will now explore more deeply.

Chapter 13

WISDOM HUMOR

I s there such a thing as a *higher humor*, humor that aligns itself with wisdom and not just knowledge? Is there a form of humor that is not simply clever and sophisticated, requiring an "inside awareness," but humor that is somehow related with a greater understanding of life? If there is, a field and a research body could be developed around this notion of *wisdom humor*.

Despite the fact that little—indeed, virtually nothing—professional has been written about humor that aligns itself with wisdom, there is a surprisingly large body of cultural and religious writing about such humor. The wise man is often depicted with a knowing smile or a frequent chuckle. Indeed, images of Gods and religious leaders have them in laughing modes quite frequently. We seem to have a notion of wisdom humor, despite the lack of professional research on the subject. I suppose it should not surprise anyone, either, that such a concept has never been given much empirical attention; it combines two aspects that have been difficult to operationalize, define, and study for centuries. If both wisdom and humor evade understanding, imagine how difficult it would be to study the combination of the two! Simply because a domain is difficult to study, however, does not mean it should be ignored or unexamined.

What Is Wisdom?

To begin, we need to be able to talk about the meaning of wisdom as it arises in distinction from knowledge. Let's consider Aristotle's notion of wisdom first. It was Aristotle (340 B.C.; 1976) who provided us with the distinction between *phronesis* (sometimes translated as "practical wisdom") and *sophia* (knowledge), which he considered a higher virtue. Phronesis is connected with action, ethics, and "particulars" whereas sophia is concerned with universal truths. In Aristotle's writings, however, it is clear that he values phronesis at least as much as sophia in that practical wisdom is what leads to "true wisdom." He focuses most of his attention on phronesis, which he believes requires a good deal of maturity and results in prudence, rational thinking, and good judgment. Political action is also dependent upon phronesis. What are the parameters of sophia, then? Aristotle only states that sophia arises as an outgrowth of the development of phronesis. It is deeper and more substantial, but he spends little time trying to define and understand sophia.

In Plato, however, we receive a much more substantial treatment of the meaning of wisdom. For Plato (375 B.C.; 1943), the wise man is one who sees the "form of the good," one who goes beyond the sensual to the higher world of forms, one who recognizes the limits of the sensual world. To use his own cave allegory (Plato, 375 B.C.; 1943), the wise man sees beyond the cave to the "real light." Here we have a knowledge not of "particulars" but of "the truth." The man who sees the form of the good possesses a kind of wisdom that is not tied to the sensual world but, rather, of a rational world of forms in which the sensual world participates. Plato's Socrates has a special kind of knowledge (Plato, 369 B.C.; 1960), then, that is beyond practical knowledge and, perhaps, most clearly distinguishes knowledge from wisdom. Socrates' claim is that he "knows that he knows nothing." Again, this is clearly not a knowledge of "particulars" but a kind of *meta-level knowledge* about one's own knowledge.

But what is it to "know that one knows nothing"? How is that any form of knowledge, let alone the highest form of knowledge, which we will call wisdom? To know that I know nothing is a kind of awareness of my own capacity. Socrates is articulating something about certainty here. He asks, in his dialogues, what courage is or what knowledge is or what virtue is—and the questioned person is always quite certain that they know what each of these is. But this definition, upon further examination, breaks down and falls apart and has all kinds of loopholes and contradictions within it—which Socrates recognizes and is able to explain. So, Platonists know that we cannot be so certain about what courage is, what knowledge is, what virtue is, etc. They are aware of the human limitations of reasoning and understanding. And this, then, becomes a fairly good definition of wisdom. The wise person *knows their own limitations.*

Perhaps this is also why wisdom is so often connected with prudence. "Not so fast," says the wise person, because one must consider all aspects of a situation before acting. Impulsive action is prone to bias, to false certainty. Even if everything appears right in the buying of a house or a car, for example, the wise person might suggest "sleeping on it," thinking it over once more, rather than acting immediately. One may not know all the facts, or one may be limited by an unknown bias. "Think again," they say, for you may find a different perspective emerges over time or with more facts available. In fact, whereas Aristotle's *phronesis* is connected with "right action," Plato's *sophia* seems more connected with meta-level knowledge and action only when it is prudent. Why? Because the sensual world can be deceptive; we are in an illusory world and often do not realize it. We are subject to a manifold of errors, biases, and mistakes. Reflect, meditate, contemplate before you act, says the wise Platonist.

Three Common Themes in Studying Wisdom

Some empirical work has been conducted on the construct "wisdom" within the psychological literature. The emphasis here has been on the *function* of wisdom, and a more Aristotelian notion of pragmatic reasoning pervades this work. Kross and Grossman (2012) identified three forms of such reasoning that comprise wisdom, all of which aid in the response to life challenges. Wisdom, according to their review, involves recognizing that the world is in flux and the future is likely to bring change and that there are limits associated with one's own knowledge. Finally, they suggest that maintaining a positive, prosocial approach that promotes the "common good" is an essential part of wisdom.

> One day, a traveling salesman was driving down a country road when he was passed by a three-legged chicken. He stepped on the gas, but at fifty miles per hour, the chicken was still ahead. After a few miles, the chicken ran up a driveway and into a barn behind an old farmhouse. The salesman drove up to the house and knocked at the door. When he told the farmer what he'd just seen, the farmer said that his son was a geneticist and had developed this breed of chicken so that he, his wife, and his son could each get a drumstick. The salesman said, "That's fantastic. How do they taste?" The farmer said, "I don't know. We can't catch 'em." (Keillor, 2005)

The twist in the story, that one can produce an improved version of a chicken for purposes of having a more substantial meal to eat but that, in the process, one loses an important trait—they that can be caught—is clearly another example of irony. How does this relate to wisdom? What is seen in this ironic twist is part of the first (and also, parenthetically, the second) aspect of wisdom outlined by Kross and Grossman. The farmer made the mistake of assuming a kind of stability of "chickenness" while striving for a better product. But the wise person who "gets the joke" here sees that one cannot assume stability, especially when one alters the nature of an aspect of reality. Of course, this also implies an assumption of the knowledge of reality (aspect two), which turns out to be false. The moral of the story is a kind of wise humility that must be maintained, for nature has its own laws and rules and changes that we humans cannot mess with. Of course, this also has an ethical dimension, if one chooses to view the story in that manner. It is a kind of justice that, in attempting to alter nature for one's own betterment, the result is a *reduction* in personal gain rather than an improvement.

Wisdom humor will, when it does manifest itself in a recognizable form, often appear in just this guile. The joke or story or life event will demonstrate what is foolish or unwise. The wisdom is then revealed in the outcome, in the seeing, in the viewing of what is foolish and the inherent recognition of the truth within the story. To recognize foolishness is to be wise. Although this may seem to be a backward or inverted method of revealing wisdom or truth, it is quite common in all revelatory stories.

> A student went to see his meditation teacher and said, "My situation is horrible! I feel so distracted most of the time, or my legs ache, or I'm repeatedly falling asleep. It's terrible."
>
> Said the teacher matter-of-factly, "It will pass."
>
> A week later, the student returned to his teacher. "My meditation is wonderful! I feel so aware, so peaceful, so alive!"
>
> "It will pass," replied the teacher. (Manku, 2008)

Again, the wise person recognizes that states of mind—good and bad, struggling or triumphing—are fleeting; they will come and go. When we interpret these in too extreme a manner, we are being foolish. The teacher here is the "steady hand" who is there to see that the sensuous world is in flux and subject to all manner of change. The permanent truths are rare and not of this world, as Plato would say. Wisdom is recognizing that. What is humorous here, though? The repetition of the identical response by the teacher is unexpected and humorous in its counterintuitive wisdom. One could easily be "taken in" by the student who first is struggling and then succeeding. But the wise person recognizes that these negative and positive states come and go without much ultimate meaning; we are mistaken when we overinterpret such states.

Let's examine the three identified aspects of wisdom in more detail. The first of these capabilities can be seen as having a kind of perspective on the nature of reality. Being aware that things are in constant flux can be traced to an early Buddhist perspective. The early Buddhists argued that the world is constantly changing and that the belief and perception of constants was an illusion. How does this sense of constant change relate to wisdom? Again, there is a tie to prudence. If one is faced with a business opportunity that appears promising at the moment, one could make a serious error, for example, by not taking into account the changing economy. The wise person has a broader perspective, considering possible changes that may occur and only choosing this opportunity if it is likely to succeed even if such changes do, in fact, take place. Only the fool acts impulsively.

> Mulla Nasrudin's face lit up as he recognized the man who was walking ahead of him down the subway stairs. He slapped the man so heartily on the back that the man nearly collapsed and cried, "Goldberg, I hardly recognized you! Why, you have gained thirty pounds since I saw you last. And you have had your nose fixed, and I swear that you are about a foot taller."
>
> The man looked at him angrily. "I beg your pardon," he said in icy tones, "but I do not happen to be Goldberg."
>
> "Aha!" said Mulla Nasrudin, "so you have even changed your name!" (Suresha, 2014)

The second aspect of wisdom outlined by Kross and Grossman harkens back to Socrates' notion of knowing one's own limits as far as knowledge goes. The fool assumes too much; the wise person recognizes that we, as humans, can only know so much and is more cautious and prudent. In this Mulla Nasrudin tale, the person refuses to recognize their own limitations and insists that their first perception—that this is their friend, Goldberg—is correct, even when the evidence mounts that this is not the case. The humor lies in Mulla's foolishness in the face of the obvious. Recognizing one's own limitations is crucial to the process of developing wisdom.

What is the nature of this epistemic limitation, though? What is it that the wise man knows and sees about human limitations that is so essential to his wisdom? This is where there is some departure. The most radical form of this is the Socratic argument that he literally knew nothing but that he knew that this was the case. On the surface, this is an explicit contradiction of reflexivity. If he knows that he knows nothing, then he no longer knows nothing. If we choose to, though, we can rescue this argument by referring to a meta-level of knowledge that has a different standing from the first type of knowledge. In that case, we can "know" that we "know nothing" because the knowledge of "knowing nothing" is not the same type of knowledge.

At any rate, wisdom can be grounded in this very radical view that we cannot know anything—or, more modestly, in the notion that we have human limitations. For example, since we cannot travel to other planets, we cannot be sure of whether life exists on these planets. Since we are still alive, we cannot say with certainty what happens after death. Acting without direct knowledge, on this more modest account, constitutes foolhardiness. Waiting to gain more perspective, knowledge, and facts before acting, in addition to recognizing human limits, constitutes wisdom.

A beautiful girl in the village was pregnant. Her angry parents demanded to know who was the father. At first resistant to confess, the anxious and embarrassed girl finally pointed to Hakuin, the Zen master whom everyone previously revered for living such a pure life. When the outraged parents confronted Hakuin with their daughter's accusation, he simply replied, "Is that so?"

When the child was born, the parents brought it to the Hakuin, who now was viewed as a pariah by the whole village. They demanded that he take care of the child since it was his responsibility. "Is that so?" Hakuin said calmly as he accepted the child.

For many months he took very good care of the child until the daughter could no longer withstand the lie she had told. She confessed that the real father was a young man in the village whom she had tried to protect. The parents immediately went to Hakuin to see if he would return the baby.

With profuse apologies, they explained what had happened. "Is that so?" Hakuin said as he handed them the child. (In5d, 2015)

The last element of wisdom identified by Kross and Grossman is a positive, prosocial view that considers the common good as a goal. In some ways, this aspect of wisdom represents a deviation from the other two in that it purports that wisdom involves action and that action has a valuation attached to it. Here the claim is made that the wise person acts in favor of the common good. Of course, this does defy some of the ordinary uses of the word "wisdom." For example, the friend who counsels their pal that, "It would be wise to keep your mouth shut about this because, if they find out that you're the culprit, you'll be in a real trouble" is not supporting the common good but only the "good for their friend," right? In fact, the connection between wisdom and "the good" can also be traced back to Platonic ideas in that knowledge, wisdom, and "the good" are always equated. Remember that, for Plato, one cannot knowingly act badly; one only acts badly out of ignorance. Knowledge is knowledge of the good, and, in that sense, the wise person's actions are always good.

In the Zen story of Master Hakuin, he chooses to forego his own ego on both the occasion of his accusation and also when the parents apologize. In the first case, we might expect a person who is concerned with self-protection, not the common good, to defend himself from the accusation. Perhaps he chooses to accept the blame and even helps to raise the child in order to save the girl from the embarrassment that she is trying to avoid. The Zen tradition would argue that forcing a person to accept the blame for something when they are not ready to do so would only cause further defensiveness and self-loathing—both impediments to development. When the parents seek forgiveness, he again chooses to emphasize the common good by not forcing them to endure greater hardship than they have already encountered with this situation. The impressiveness of the master's gesture is even greater considering his standing as "master" and the fact that he is being publicly embarrassed in front of his own students.

The humor here, of course, is rooted in his use of the very same expression in each case: "Is that so?" The neutrality of that articulation and its lack of affect are unexpected in this circumstance and therefore humorous. When repeated in an equally emotional moment in the opposite direction—being vindicated rather than accused—it becomes even more humorous. But this is also a wisdom tale because of the master's transcendence of the ego and his insistence on helping others, even at the cost of his own reputation.

The common good, of course, is the key factor here that makes this element a moral dimension and not just an epistemic one. There does seem to be some face validity to the claim that there is a connection between wisdom and good, prosocial action. Think of a counterexample. We might claim, for example, that Hannibal Lecter, the evil genius psychopath, is clever, is a genius, or is even brilliant—but we would not, generally, say that he is "wise." Wisdom does seem to be reserved for those who act in favor of the common good or at least "think" in terms of the common good.

We do, however, speak of "wise investments" that only benefit the investor—but I'm not sure we'd ascribe the trait of "wisdom" to the profit-seeking investor. Knowledge that promotes good for only one person and has no regard for the common good would not be properly called wisdom.

Measures of Wisdom as a Trait

As already indicated, wisdom has received very little research attention until fairly recently. Within the last 20 years, however, two measures have emerged as relatively reliable and valid measures of the personality trait, wisdom. The Self-Assessed Wisdom Scale (Webster, 2007) stands as perhaps the most sophisticated measure proposed in the literature. Webster's scale is comprised of five factors—openness, emotional regulation, humor, critical life experiences, and reflection. Most noteworthy here is the conceptualization of humor as a major component of wisdom. Webster argues that the wise individual recognizes, enjoys, and utilizes humor in a variety of contexts and for a myriad of reasons. He claims that humor/comedy is likely to be recognized and used by the wise person because of the twists and turns and ironies that life presents.

In the scale itself, however, the items that relate to humor have more to do with the use of humor in social settings and for one's social relations—"I can make fun of myself to comfort others" and "I often use humor to put others at ease." Perhaps there is some rather considerable *value* in this use of humor for we know from other work (Martin, 2007) that humor is a very good social tool for establishing and promoting good social standing and positive relationships. But is this what we mean by true wisdom? Unfortunately, Webster does not report correlations between this single factor and his dependent or criterion variables. He has looked at a number of variables, such as attachment anxiety, close relationships, and age. Interestingly, according to his work, wisdom does not increase with age; it appears to act more like a permanent personality variable that does not change over time. Again, we have to question whether this has face validity in that it seems that wisdom ought to develop, at least slightly, over a person's lifetime.

The other prominent measure of wisdom that has been proposed is called the Three-Dimensional Wisdom Scale (Ardelt, 2003), and it was designed specifically for use with aging populations. The three dimensions of wisdom proposed are cognitive, reflective, and affective components. Little work has been conducted on this relatively new scale. Research by Taylor et al. (2011) suggests that the three-dimensional scale may have some serious psychometric weaknesses. The idea, however, that wisdom has more than simply a cognitive component is fruitful both for the study of wisdom in general and for the study of something like wisdom humor, since humor is often immediate and affective, rather than purely cognitive.

Thus far, no studies have been conducted using measures of wisdom and sense of humor. One could, perhaps, explore this relationship empirically to determine what the relationship is between the development of wisdom and one's sense of humor. Specifically, the following hypotheses could be tested: 1) Do wiser people use humor more in their everyday life? This might mean both the reception of humor and the initiation of comedy in their social experience, 2) Do wise people have different senses of humor from those who are not wise? For example, do wise people prefer higher forms of humor such as irony and wisdom humor over more base humor such as physical—aggression humor, insults, and sarcasm? 3) Would higher forms of humor be understood better and appreciated more by wise individuals than by unwise people?

Humility as Wisdom

The Emperor of China was delighted to meet one of the great Buddhist monks and teachers, Bodhidharma. On meeting

> Bodhidharma, the Emperor is said to have asked, "I have built many temples, copied innumerable Sutras, and ordained many monks since becoming Emperor. Therefore, I ask you, what is my merit?"
>
> "None whatsoever!" answered Bodhidharma.
>
> "Why no merit?" asked the Emperor.
>
> Bodhidharma replied, "Doing things for merit has an impure motive and will only bear the puny fruit of rebirth."
>
> The Emperor was a little put off, and then asked, "What, then, is the most important principle of Buddhism?"
>
> Bodhidharma replied, "Vast emptiness. Nothing sacred."
>
> The Emperor, now bewildered, and not a little indignant, then asked, "Who is this that stands before me?"
>
> Bodhidharma replied, "I don't know." (McCrae, 2003, p. 22)

This is probably one of the more straightforward Buddhist tales, with its emphasis on humility and the doctrine of "no-self" at the core of this dialogue. But it is also humorous in a very classic manner. The Emperor appears as this very stuffy, pompous individual who wishes his own "good deeds" would lead to some tangible reward or recognition from the spiritual master. In some ways, his persona reminds one of some of the foils in the early Charlie Chaplin movies or in the Marx Brothers films in which those inflated egos are ridiculed or embarrassed. The Buddhist master, however, takes the role of "the wise fool," allowing the Emperor to make a narcissistic fool of himself repeatedly, with a final punchline that is quite absurd but also sensible and noble. "I don't know" is certainly an unexpected response to the question of what one's name is, but, of course, it serves the purpose of highlighting the Buddhist doctrine of "no-self" in that one should not take oneself seriously as a particular being. You can almost picture the Emperor's frustration through the course of the dialogue in physical terms—his face getting red, his sticking his chest out indignantly, and challenging the master with an increasingly threatening tone. All of this leads to a comedic tone to the story.

Is this really humor, though, or simply an enlightening story that reminds us of the value of humility? I would argue that there is humor inherent in the insight that is revealed in each case but that a knowing smile, a small chuckle, or a couple of *ha-has* is about all that we might expect. Leave it to the neuropsychologists to determine the physical correlates of such responses, but I would suggest that they may be substantial in terms of the effect on mood and temperament. This is why these "tales" are so integral to many religious teachings. Reading the biblical stories or listening to the master tell these kinds of stories is a central part of the training of the young student or monk within these religious traditions.

Yamaoka Tesshu, a samurai and student of Zen, traveled around Japan studying from various Zen masters. One day, he wandered into the Shokoku Temple and happened upon the monk Dokuon. In a desire to show his comprehension of Zen, Tesshu stated to the Master, "The mind, the Buddha, and all beings are empty. The true nature of all things is emptiness. There is no enlightenment, no delusion; no sages, no commoners; no toil, no reward."

Master Dokuon remained quiet for some time and then banged him on the head. Tesshu fumed in anger and asked, "What did you do that for?"

Master Dokuon replied, "If everything is empty, where did the temper come from?" (Isha Institute, 2021)

This tale reveals the important difference between intellectual knowledge and more full-bodied, experiential knowledge or wisdom. The swordsman says all the right things—about the doctrine of emptiness and no-self. He announces it triumphantly, though, which provides a hint that he, himself, is ego-attached to his knowledge in a way that, ironically, contradicts the doctrine itself. It is akin to one seeking recognition for being uninterested in recognition. The master, then, is able to approach this situation and break through to the student only with his action—physically striking the student, which inspires anger. Humor arises here because of the irony of the student's pretense of knowing while he still responds, emotionally, with a primitive anger that reveals his lack of "real" wisdom. Another aspect of the humor here is the physicality of the teachings; one would not expect a religious teacher to use brute force in getting his point across. The comedic aspect of the story is rescued by the fact that no real damage is done, presumably, and the student is forced to reflect on the true state of his knowledge.

What is wisdom humor, then? Are these three elements of wisdom always portrayed in it? It seems that many virtues are portrayed in examples of wisdom humor. The three identified in empirical work, thus far—awareness of constant change, recognition of the limits of human knowledge, and the execution of good deeds—are useful as a beginning point but are probably just scratching the surface of the essence of wisdom and elements that can, ultimately, be portrayed in wisdom humor. In our reflections here, we have also developed categories of humility and prudence. Many other forms of wisdom may be manifested in this form of humor, as well.

One of the striking aspects of wisdom humor is that, as the terminus in forms of humor, this form of humor provides a kind of "final transcendence" of the human project. There is no further action to be taken, story to be told, or mountain to climb. A Sufi tale might help illustrate this point:

> There was once a small boy who banged a drum all day and loved every moment of it. He would not be quiet, no matter what anyone else said or did. Various people who called themselves Sufis, and other well-wishers, were called in by neighbors and asked to do something about the child. The first so-called Sufi told the boy that he would, if he continued to make noise,

perforate his eardrums; this reasoning was too advanced for the child, who was neither a scientist nor a scholar. The second told him that drum beating was a sacred activity and should be carried out only on special occasions. The third offered the neighbors plugs for their ears; the fourth gave the boy a book; the fifth gave the neighbors books that described methods of controlling their anger; the sixth gave the boy meditation exercises to make him placid and explained that all reality was an illusion. All of these remedies worked for a short while, but none worked for very long. Eventually, a real Sufi came along. He looked at the situation, handed the boy a hammer and chisel and said, "I wonder what is *inside* the drum?" (Shah, 1978)

This final solution of creating curiosity in the boy about the *inside* of the drum represents a kind of "aha wisdom humor moment." It is symbolic because all the other solutions were, in a sense, dealing with the external aspects of the situation but not the internal situation. None of them involved using the child's own curiosity and fascination with the drum but, instead, treated the child as if he was just a nuisance. Moreover, the "true Sufi" expresses his own curiosity, not a proposed solution. They *enter into the situation with the child* rather than opposing him from outside. Finally, the wise solution provides a complete solution; once the drum is broken, it can no longer be played. All other proposed solutions were temporary and incomplete.

A master ordered the young monk, "Go and buy some fruits for me. Make sure they're sweet."

"Yes, master," said the monk.

The monk went to the market and found a fruit dealer who exclaimed, "All of my fruits are sweet and juicy. If you don't believe me, try one."

The monk decided that, to make sure all of the fruits he

was buying were sweet, he would try every single piece of fruit. "Master, I've made sure that all the fruits I bought were sweet." (Lim, 1995, p. 144)

This Zen parable plays on a conflict between certainty, on the one hand, and intrusion on the other. To be absolutely certain that each fruit is ripe, you would have to bite into each piece—but, of course, that ruins the fruit for the eventual consumer of the fruit. The parable focuses on this humorous contradiction between knowing and the in-itself of the object. Knowing ruptures the in-itself nature of the object. In one way, this is a story of a foolish attempt to satisfy the master—one that is obviously not satisfying. But the monk also reveals the conflict within the master's demand to "make sure the fruits are sweet." Of course, we sensible people would compromise, asking to "test" a couple of the fruits but not all the fruit purchased. But, in fact, the monk was right, and that is what the crux of the humor is: In order to *really know* if a piece of fruit is, indeed, sweet, you would have to taste it!

There was a man who was blessed with the Five Gifts (special sight, hearing, and other unusual abilities). He had a pair of special eyes that could see treasures buried in the ground. The emperor said, "If we can make him stay in our country, we'll be rich."

Some servants overheard this conversation and decided upon a solution. They attacked the special man and proudly reported back to the Emperor, "Your Majesty, I've gouged out the eyes of that man. From now on, he can never go anywhere else." (Lim, 1995, p. 72)

Again, the *solution* utilized serves to resolve one of the issues at hand but incurs a negative, which negates the positive of that solution. If the man cannot see, he cannot leave, but he also no longer has any special powers of seeing. What this Zen parable reveals is the classic "two sides of the same coin" concept that is central to nearly all Eastern wisdom. The pursuit of the pure positive—wealth, in this case—is fraught with contradiction. Good and bad are intimately tied to each other. Of course, here the desire to use another for one's own personal gain (or even the country's) is seen as egoistic so there is also a moral dimension to this story. The Emperor does not profit, in the end (although one cannot help but wonder why they didn't chop off his legs instead, but that would not make for a very good Zen parable).

Wisdom Humor in the Bible?

Thus far, we have considered many tales and stories, labeled here as wisdom humor tales, from Eastern traditions. It seems that the Zen and Sufi traditions have a propensity for doling out wisdom through jokes or humorous stories that reveal truths about life. What about the Western tradition? Surely there must be examples of humor—and especially wisdom humor—in the Bible?

This has been a matter of some controversy among humor scholars. Beginning with a famous statement by Alfred North Whitehead that, "The lack of humor in the Bible is one of the singular things in all literature" (1954; 2001), many have attempted to address this question of the role of humor in the Bible. A lively debate broke out in the *International Journal of Humor Research* in which Friedman (2000) argued that there is much humor in the Old Testament and even provided more than 100 examples of such humor. John Morreall (2001), of William & Mary, disputed Friedman's contentions, though, showing that, though there is certainly wordplay, sarcasm, and irony in the Bible, there is a lack of real humor. All the examples Friedman provided, Morreall claimed, are without humor in the sense of enjoyable mirth. Morreall concluded, "The only laughter attributed to God in the Bible is this last kind: God laughs only in scorn, not amusement or mirth" (p. 300, 2001).

Unfortunately, we must conclude, with Morreall, that this true. The Bible's God is not one who laughs with wisdom but only with scorn at those who have betrayed Him or have lived a life as sinners and will soon suffer a negative fate at His hands. There is irony in the Bible but not comedic irony, only tragic irony. Friedman's example of 250 people being drowned by God fits nicely here. This is ironic but not funny.

But is the Judeo-Christian world devoid of humor? Not at all. The wise Christian or Jew can find humorous many of the same stories we've presented in this chapter. They, too, would have some of the same values of prudence, humility, and self-understanding. Tales of youth being impetuous or naive could count just as easily as Christian wisdom as it does Eastern wisdom. But the Bible, as Whitehead alluded to, is simply not a comedy, but more of a tragic story. The Bible provides stories that could be laughed at, certainly; there are many tales of foolishness, naivety, and poor judgment at which we can laugh. But that does not seem to be the tone and tenor of the manuscript. It is intended as a doctrine for us to "take heed" and "hear the warnings" and "abide by the law" and "come to God," not as a set of humorous tales for us to decipher in order to reach a level of wisdom or understanding.

Why, then, is wisdom humor so prevalent in the Eastern traditions such as Buddhism and Zen Buddhism, in particular? The goal of Zen Buddhism is to reach *satori*, which is defined as "sudden insight." This sudden insight is promoted by meditation and inquiry with the *roshi* (teacher). The student or monk is asked to contemplate, directly or indirectly, the nature of reality, the status of the self, the meaning of life—with the eventual goal of recognizing that one was living in an illusory reality that was promulgated by discursive consciousness. Zen tales, stories, and riddles—filled with contradictions, ironies, and humor—are utilized to aid in this process of recognizing this illusion and *breaking through to the truth* about reality, the self, and the nature of consciousness. Wisdom is, therefore, married to humor, and this humor serves as part of the process of reaching *satori* or enlightenment.

Humor, as we have seen, relies upon the unexpected, the twists and turns that life presents, and provides new ways of looking at life situations. The development of the Zen student is predicated on *seeing* in new ways and recognizing one's own epistemic limitations. In some ways, we can say that the Buddhist tradition focuses more on the cognitive aspects of developing awareness whereas the Judeo-Christian tradition is much more focused on "right action." Acting according to God's law and with humility and consideration is what "gets you to heaven," rather than an epistemic breakthrough in which you overcome illusion.

Although there are few examples, if any, of wisdom humor in the Bible, one possible such example that has been cited is the story of the Prodigal Son.

There once was a man who had two grown sons. When the younger son asked for a share of the property, the father divided his estate. The older son stayed and worked hard on the farm, while the younger son took his share, turned it into cash, and set off for a distant country.

The younger son spent his time and money on loose living until, at last, all his wealth was squandered. As a great famine descended upon the land, the younger son was without shelter or food. Pangs of hunger drove him to seek employment. He went to work as a swineherd for a local farmer. Each day as he tossed the pigs their carob pods, he realized that the pigs were better fed than he. He thought, *Even the lowest servants in my father's house have bread to spare.*

He decided to return home and beg his father to take him in as a servant. He thought, *I will say that I have sinned against heaven and before my father. I am not worthy to be a son.*

As the contrite young man approached his family home, his

father saw him at a distance and ran out to greet him. He compassionately threw his arms around the boy and kissed him. The son said, "Father, I am not worthy to be your son. Consider me as a servant. I have sinned before heaven and before you."

But the father called to his servants, "Bring the best robe! Bring shoes fit for a free man, not a servant! Kill the fatted calf, prepare a feast, and make merry! My son was lost, but now he is found!"

The father led his son to a celebration of his return. There was music and dancing and merrymaking.

Meanwhile, the elder son returned home from his work on the family farm and heard the music and dancing. As he approached the house, he asked one of the servants the meaning of the celebration. The servant told him how his father joyously celebrated his younger brother's safe return.

The older brother's face flushed crimson with rage. He refused to go into the house. His father came out to entreat him to join the festivities. The son stubbornly protested, "All these years I have loyally served you, never disobeying your command. You did not give me a party! Yet this spendthrift son of yours, who wandered away and squandered the family money on vice and bawdy living, is lavishly celebrated! Why?"

The father smiled warmly at his bristling son and explained, "My celebration of your brother's return takes away none of the love I have for you. Everything I have is already yours! As for all this merrymaking—I delight in the return of my wayward son. It is as if your brother had been dead but came back to life. He was gone, but now he is found. This is indeed a reason to rejoice!" (Forest, 1996, p. 87–88)

The parable of the Prodigal Son is, at the most, only slightly humorous. The humor rests with the irony of the older son, who is loyal, hardworking, and disciplined—yet he fails to get the attention and recognition that the younger, prodigal son receives. The younger one, in fact, lives a life of pleasure—up to a point, at least—and yet manages to stay in the good graces of the father, despite his transgressions.

The structure of this story mimics that of many of the Zen and other Eastern parables we've considered. Good and evil are intimately tied together. The older son is hardworking and loyal but, therefore, never gets the full attention, respect, and admiration he craves from the father. The prodigal son is decadent and impulsive, leading to a ruinous life, but winds up getting much love and attention from the father. But a key factor here is probably the *attitude* of the younger, prodigal son upon returning. He asks for nothing, is humble, and is even willing to forgo his status as "son." This, in a Christian context, allows the father to accept him and welcome him. If he had demanded his status be granted, the story would be different; the father's acceptance might not be understandable. Is this story humorous, though? Of course, to some extent, that depends on the reader, but I would say, compromising between the positions of Friedman and Morreall, slightly so. It can bring a chuckle as one considers the irony of working hard and never being fully appreciated in contrast with the prodigal son who lives a carefree, aesthetic life and is welcomed and appreciated.

> Long ago in India, there lived a vain and ferocious lion. He roamed the jungle and killed for pleasure. To show his power, he killed more animals than he needed to eat. The animals lived in terror of this beast. One day they gathered to decide how they might peacefully persuade the lion to end his evil ways. They agreed that each day, one animal would offer to be the lion's meal. Armed with this brave plan, the animals approached the ferocious lion.
>
> "O Lion, king of the jungle," they cried, "if you will stop your unnecessary killing, we have agreed to send one animal each day

to be your supper. Think of it! You will live a life of leisure. You will never need to hunt again. One animal each day shall come willingly to your den."

The lion considered the plan and, to everyone's surprise, roared, "I agree to this plan! The creature who is to be my dinner must come at the proper time. I do not like to wait for my meals!"

The next day the animals sent a wise old rabbit to be the lion's meal. As the rabbit went along the road to the lion's den, he walked very slowly. He dawdled here and there along the way, nibbling at leaves and conversing with friends. By the time the rabbit arrived at the lion's den, it was very late in the day. The sun was setting, and the lion was ravenous.

"Why are you late?" he roared. "You've made me wait!"

"Your Majesty," said the rabbit, "it is true that I am late. However, I am not to blame. A wicked, ferocious lion prevented me from arriving on time. I can picture him now. He had long, sharp claws like yours, a swishing tail like yours, frightening teeth, and a huge mane like yours."

The lion when into a rage. "Another lion in my jungle? Take me to him!"

"I can easily bring you to him," said the rabbit. "Come, and I will show you the lion."

The clever rabbit led the lion to a deep well filled with water. He pointed down into the well and said, "Look, Your Majesty, and you will see the most wicked lion in the jungle."

The lion walked to the well, looked down into it, and saw his own reflection in the water. Thinking it was another lion, he roared a terrible roar: "R-O-A-RRR!"

The sound of his roar filled the well and bounced back to him as an echo. "R-O-A-RRR!"

"Who are you?" he roared even louder.

His echo answered, "Who are you?"

"I am the king of this jungle!" he roared again.

His echo answered, "I am the king of this jungle!"

"How dare you call yourself the king?" he roared with even greater fury.

His echo answered, "How dare you call yourself the king?"

This was more than the proud lion could bear. He became so enraged that with claws spread wide and sharp teeth showing, he charged into the deep well with a great splash!

The wise old rabbit went back to the other animals to tell them how the wicked lion had violently attacked his own reflection—and would never be heard from again. (from Forest, 1996, p. 23–24)

This tale has its origin in the Panchatantra, an ancient Indian collection of stories that is believed to have been composed in the 3rd century. It provides a wonderful contrast between blind desire and ego with clever wisdom. The wise rabbit uses the lion's own ego against himself. What is particularly striking is the wonderful imagery of the well, which provides a mirror for the lion to "see himself," which winds up leading to his demise. In one sense, this highlights the one aspect that is most lacking in the lion: he doesn't reflect on himself but only acts on his impulses. Once he does reflect, by virtue of the rabbit's clever trick, he is unable to carry on with his evil ways.

Is this tale funny, though? Well, it is, in the sense that we can laugh in a celebratory fashion "at" the lion's demise, in the end. The laughter may also be in consonance with the wise rabbit, who outfoxed the beast of the jungle. We (the reader undoubtedly identifies with the other animals, against the lion) have transcended the lion and overcome his reign of terror by turning him on himself, without any further loss from our own ranks. This is also a kind of "victory humor," a victory of reason over pure desire—or reason over foolishness.

The often-cited tale "The Emperor's New Clothes" (Andersen et al., 1949) can also be considered a wisdom humor story. Hans Christian Andersen took an old folktale and created this cautionary tale. In it, the emperor is described as a narcissist and clothes fanatic. He employs some highly regarded weavers to create an outfit that is fine and beautiful but also contains a magical element. If a person who was not fit for their position or simply foolish, they would not see the clothes at all. The emperor is delighted by the proposition! He believes that he will be able to detect those who are unfit for their positions by their reaction to this outfit.

> The Emperor undressed, and the swindlers pretended to put his new clothes on him, one garment after another. They took him around the waist and seemed to be fastening something—that was his train—as the Emperor turned round and round before the looking glass.
>
> "How well Your Majesty's new clothes look. Aren't they becoming?" He heard on all sides, "That pattern, so perfect! Those colors, so suitable! It is a magnificent outfit." (Andersen et al., 1949, p. 25)

Everyone, including the Emperor, was afraid to remark that there was no fabric, nothing at all—because they knew that they would be regarded as foolish or unfit for their position. The weavers were charlatans, taking advantage of people's insecurities—since everyone fears that perhaps they are unfit for their position or a simpleton.

> The noblemen who were to carry his train stooped low and reached for the floor as if they were picking up his mantle. Then they pretended to lift and hold it high. They didn't dare admit they had nothing to hold.
>
> So off went the Emperor in procession under his splendid

canopy. Everyone in the streets and the windows said, "Oh, how fine are the Emperor's new clothes! Don't they fit him to perfection? And see his long train!" Nobody would confess that he couldn't see anything, for that would prove him either unfit for his position or a fool. No costume the Emperor had worn before was ever such a complete success.

"But he hasn't got anything on," a little child said.

"Did you ever hear such innocent prattle?" said the child's father. And one person whispered to another what the child had said, "He hasn't anything on. A child says he hasn't anything on."

"But he hasn't got anything on!" the whole town cried out at last.

The Emperor shivered, for he suspected they were right. But he thought, *This procession has got to go on.* So he walked more proudly than ever, as his noblemen held high the train that wasn't there at all. (Andersen et al., p. 32)

What is most curious and, in fact, humorous about the tale is that the one who is willing to blurt out the most obvious truth is a child. Of course, this is a fairly common motif in wisdom tales, that innocence proves to be a form of wisdom. The child sees no clothes on the Emperor and is not hampered by their own insecurities or doubts. They proclaim the truth in a straightforward manner. The Emperor, on the other hand, proves to be as foolish or, perhaps, even more foolish than the everyday person. The townsfolk are then inspired by the child to recognize and acknowledge the plain truth. But the Emperor is so caught up in his own need to be superior and his assistants are also entangled in their own needs to retain their positions, so they assuage the Emperor's fears by playing along with the fantasy. If there is a moral here, it is that one may be so blinded by one's own needs that they convince themselves of a reality that is illusory. Wisdom comes in the form of a direct perception of the plain truth—which the child, in their innocence, is able to provide.

There once was a teacher who lived with a great number of students in a run-down temple. The students supported themselves by begging for food in the bustling streets of a nearby town. Some of the students grumbled about their humble living conditions. In response, the old master said one day, "We must repair the walls of this temple. Since we occupy ourselves with study and meditation, there is no time to earn the money we will need. I have thought of a simple solution."

All the students eagerly gathered closer to hear the words of their teacher. The master said, "Each of you must go into the town and steal goods that can be sold for money. In this way, we will be able to do the good work of repairing our temple."

The students were startled at this suggestion from their wise master. But since they respected him greatly, they assumed he must have good judgment and did not protest.

The wise master said sternly, "In order not to defile our excellent reputation by committing illegal and immoral acts, please be certain to steal when no one is looking. I do not want anyone to be caught."

When the teacher walked away, the students discussed the plan amongst themselves. "It is wrong to steal," said one. "Why has our wise master asked us to do this?"

Another retorted, "It will allow us to build our temple, which is a good result."

They all agreed that their teacher was wise and just and must have a sensible reason for making such an unusual request. They set out eagerly for the town, promising each other that they would not disgrace their school by getting caught. "Be careful," they called to one another. "Do not let anyone see you stealing."

All the students except one young boy set forth. The wise master approached him and asked, "Why do you stay behind?"

The boy responded, "I cannot follow your instructions to

steal where no one will see me. Wherever I go, *I* am always there watching. My *own* eyes will see me steal."

The wise master tearfully embraced the boy. "I was just testing the integrity of my students," he said. "You are the only one who has passed the test." The boy went on to become a great teacher himself. (Khan, 1939)

There are several morals to this Jataka tale, which probably dates from the 4th century B.C. One of the themes has been prominently studied in modern social psychology—that of obedience. The students who carried out the master's orders did so with blind obedience, even though they had serious reservations about committing the transgressions. Perhaps this serves as an ancient example of obedience to authority, which was demonstrated so powerfully in the Milgram experiment (Milgram, 1963) in which subjects were willing to give electric shocks at an alarming level to other peers participating in the experiment. Of course, the Milgram study was "rigged" with a confederate playing the role of another subject and no real shock was imposed. The wise student here is heroic in that he *thinks for himself* and is unwilling to carry out the unethical commands of the master.

But the notion of "seeing oneself" is, once again, critical in this wisdom tale. The master exhorts his students to "not be seen" as they commit these acts, knowing full well that this is impossible. The student's task is to recognize this impossibility, but only one student is mature enough to know this. Wisdom lies in this inability to carry out the master's orders, but also in the master's strategy itself, as it provides an excellent acid test of the student's development. What is the humor here, though? Remember that wisdom humor is, generally, not going to engender a deep belly laugh or a loud outburst but, rather, an "aha" chuckle, and this tale certainly can produce this sort of reaction. We're laughing at the twist in the story—that this was a test given by the master that only the wisest student could pass. We're also acknowledging the truth of the good student's response, "One sees oneself at every moment." And perhaps we're laughing at the unexpected reversal involved in the correct response to the master's command being that of defiance or refusal.

The king's son was so sad that his eyes forever threatened a downpour of tears. In the palace, servants catered to his every need. The cooks prepared the tastiest dishes for him. Toy makers created the cleverest playthings. Tutors shared their most stimulating ideas. Yet he remained sullen and sad.

The king cherished the boy and wished only for his happiness. Finally, unable to bear the prince's despair a moment longer, the king called for advisers from far and wide to study the situation and provide a solution to the prince's sorrow. After much stargazing, consideration, and calculation, the wise counselors decreed, "You must dress the prince in the shirt of a truly happy man, and he will be cured of his sorrow."

Delighted with this simple solution, the king set out on a journey to find a truly happy man whose shirt would make his son happy again. With a great retinue he traveled to a nearby town where there lived a pious priest whose radiant smile cheered and comforted the heart of everyone he met. Because the priest was known to be a happy man, the king went directly to his home. The priest greeted the king with a humble bow. "To what do I owe this honor, Your Majesty?" asked the priest.

The king replied, "Since you are so revered for your holiness and good nature, I would like to know if you would accept the position of bishop, would it be offered to you?"

The priest smiled happily and replied, "Most certainly!"

The king frowned and said to himself, with a sigh, "This man's shirt will not do. He is not truly happy. If he were truly happy, he would want no more than what he already has."

The king journeyed on to another land where lived a sultan whose kingdom was peaceful and whose people were content. The visiting king was welcomed with a royal feast. At the dinner, the visiting king said to the sultan, "You seem to be a happy man. What makes you so?"

The sultan replied, "I have everything I could possibly want and truly want no more. Yet late at night as I fall asleep, I worry about losing all I have worked so hard to gain."

Once again, the king sighed and said to himself, "This man's shirt will not do."

In place after place, the king searched but could not find a man who was truly content with his life. The king was about to give up the quest when he happened to be riding across a vineyard and heard the most joyous singing. In the distance, he saw a poor farmer who was harvesting his grapes and singing at the top of his lungs in a voice that rivaled the birds. The king approached the peasant, who turned with a smile and said, "Good day!"

The king climbed down off his horse and walked toward the man. "You seem so happy today," said the king.

The man replied, "Indeed I am, every day. I am blessed with a wonderful life!"

The king said, "Your smile is so radiant. Come with me to the royal castle. You will be surrounded with luxury and never want for anything again."

The man munched a grape and said, "No, thank you. I would not give up my life for all the castles in the world."

The king could not contain his joy. "My son is saved! My son is saved!" he shouted. "Please, you must do something for your king!"

The man bowed and said, "Anything you wish, Your Majesty."

The king reached out and, opening the farmer's ragged jacket, shouted, "You must give me your shirt!"

The king's eyes stared wide with astonishment at the sight of the young man's muscular chest. The truly happy man was not wearing a shirt. (in Forest, 1996, p. 117–119)

Believed to have its source in Italy, "The Happy Man's Shirt" is an interesting tale that contains both wisdom and humor. There is certainly irony in the surprise ending—that, when the king finally succeeds in finding a happy man, he has no shirt to offer. The wisdom, of course, is connected with the dialectic between *having* and *being*. The prince already has everything he wants, and what he doesn't have, the king will give him if he simply asks for it. But he is not content because he doesn't know who he is or has no real meaning in his life. Everything is offered to him, but he knows that nothing that is procured will satisfy him. We might say that he is existentially unhappy.

The imagery of the shirt is a curious blend. The shirt, in one way, stands for the man. It clings to his body, even covering his most precious organs (heart, lungs, etc.). If the king can find a happy man, that happiness can be transferred by the medium of the shirt. In the end, though, the shirt, too, turns out to be external and not essential. The twist that the happy man has no shirt, in fact, is what comprises both the wisdom and, in fact, the humor in the story. He *is* his happiness rather than *possessing it* in some external way. There is no way to transfer his happiness to another.

The humor in this story comes from our "buying into" the notion of the shirt being the key to the prince's happiness. Although we naturally find this notion of taking the happy man's shirt being a solution to the prince's plight absurd and ridiculous, we are taken into this presumption and accept it. But the surprise twist in the end is that this assumption, in fact, was illusory. Not everyone has a shirt; in fact, the happy man has no shirt!

Wisdom humor not only serves as the highest level of humor, but its existence should provide some guidance regarding our ultimate question—the nature of humor itself. Humor, in this case, does not require a belly laugh or any form of giddiness but only a knowing smile. Wisdom, moreover, cannot be given at birth but requires living in the spatial/temporal world and learning the lessons of life. The knowing smile, then, is acquired as a result of both life lessons and also a kind of attention to what life brings. In fact, wisdom, by its very nature, means learning from experience and not mindlessly repeating foolish mistakes. Eckhart Tolle (2016) says about laughter that, "It's very liberating—particularly to laugh at the human condition and to laugh at one's own mind-patterns because it implies that you've taken one step back, to retreat, and have seen your own patterns or your own drama that's produced by your mind-patterns—and when you recognize drama as drama, it becomes funny."

Wisdom Humor and Personality

What kind of person would most appreciate wisdom humor? Our first inclination would be to point to those with a spiritual point of view. Of course, we wouldn't expect that those whose primary motivations are toward power, wealth, or revenge would be able to appreciate wisdom humor. But would the enlightened person be engaging in this form of humor, or would it more likely be those who desire or seek greater wisdom, truth, and knowledge acknowledging such a lack within themselves? I believe that the person on a spiritual path or seeking to expand their understanding of life would be most interested in this form of humor. Moreover, to appreciate this form of humor, one would perhaps need to hold humility, patience, and compassion as core values. Wisdom humor can certainly function as one of the tools on the path of spiritual development.

Conclusion

WHAT IS HUMOR?
CONCLUDING THOUGHTS

The central question in this book has consistently been "What is humor?" In one way, this question cannot be answered—because an answer to the question of what something is must not contain the element in question within it. Humor, then, must be described by things other than humor—but there is nothing, other than humor, that can really describe humor. Some have resorted to the concept that humor is "play" of a certain sort. But there are many kinds of play, some of which clearly do not involve humor. There is a temptation to reduce humor to a biological phenomenon, in which case they may focus on brain wave patterns, chemical reactions, or physiological behaviors that are associated with humor and laughing. But this is not really answering the question we have set out to explore. Humor is a perception, not a physiological reaction.

One of the most compelling answers to the question of what humor is was offered by Robert Hariman (2007) of Northwestern University. He argues that humor is a sudden change of state of mind that is pleasurable. Despite the fact that this is largely true, descriptively, we can still think of many examples of pleasurable changes of states of mind that do not involve humor—so how can that serve as a definition or characterization of humor? When one is surprised by an old friend's presence, for example, a change of state occurs that is quite pleasurable, but there may not be any particular humor or comedy involved. In fact, if the excitement is really great, the person who sees their long-lost friend might weep tears of joy—hardly connected to humor.

Another approach to the question of what humor is focuses on its connection with "the truth." Seinfeld speaks about this in one of his conversations. He argues that humor is not the same as truth. "Funny is funny. Funny has a certain life to it, a certain magic to it. If you only needed truth, people would just read the paper and howl." (Seinfeld, 2018)

The Opposite of Humor: Taking Life Seriously

One method by which one can define or understand something is to consider its opposite. A thing is what it is by virtue of it not being what it is not, after all. If we were to consider the opposite of humor, we would be forced to think about what it means to "take something seriously." To be serious about something is to obliterate all possibility of humor entering into the equation. Being serious means not allowing oneself to poke fun at, laugh at, or make light of whatever one is "taking seriously."

What, then, is it to take something seriously? One immediate observation is that taking something seriously is taking it at "face value." To use an overused modern expression, "It is what it is." One sees it for what it is and is not immune to the consequences of that reality. "This is serious" is often a way of saying, "There will be consequences," and therefore one cannot or should not "make light of it" or "joke about it."

This does serve to, once again, reaffirm our continued observation that humor is only really possible when there are no serious consequences involved in the situation. Humor depends on no serious consequences occurring—otherwise, we'd be forced to "take it seriously." Humor, then, is light and free of consequence.

Humor Is Indefinable

Ultimately, humor is indefinable. Our own understanding of humor as "transcendence" is, perhaps, most universalizable but still not satisfactory because that which is particularly characterized by humor eludes definition. It is not like any other thing but, rather, is an entity unto itself. We are, therefore, always tempted to place "humor" or "comedy" into the definition of humor—while knowing that this violates a basic rule that one cannot define something with itself. For example, humor is said to be the perception of incongruity that leads to laughter. Again, the problem is that many other emotions may result from the perception of incongruity. A person might be bewildered, angry, surprised, disconcerted, or just confused. The addition of the laughter in the equation is essentially "cheating," because that implies humor in the definition.

To define humor, we would have to refer to something that is not humor but which somehow is akin to or related to humor. To define humor, we would need other words for the concept of humor. But to articulate the point one more time, *there is simply nothing like humor*. We can say a great deal about it, but we cannot really define it in terms other than itself.

Consider a person who is completely humorless. I don't mean your current boss or a person whose sense of humor is limited or primitive or weak—but one who has no access to humor whatsoever. How could you explain to them what humor is, such that they would be able to engage in it? It would be impossible. You could point to incongruities, ironies, surprise endings, or even resort to tickling them—but to no end. Humor cannot be arrived at from outside of it.

Humor is associated with laughter, certain kinds of feelings, and most definitely certain brain states. But what is it that we are doing when we are laughing at something? The best answer we can give is that humor is a kind of transcendence. It is a "moving beyond" the moment, the situation, the predicament, or the dilemma a person faces. It temporarily frees the person of that situation by allowing one to transcend it in humor. Of course, we fall victim to a similar problem we encountered with the proposal that humor is, essentially, "play" with this new definition. There are many ways to transcend the moment, humor being only one of them. How, then, can humor be transcendence only? It is not.

Humor as Knowing

There is also most definitely an epistemological aspect of humor. We often use the expression "a knowing smile" to indicate that one both knows something and is able to laugh at the situation. In that moment of transcendence is a knowing moment, where the person is outside and looking in. Conversely, we saw the pain and suffering that can be caused by "being seen" in the moment of being laughed at. The stakes are high in humor because of the wide range between the exaltation of laughing at and the ridicule of being laughed at. Knowing is the crucial element here. The laughing one knows something; those laughed at are seen as inside something and suffer the pain of such.

What, then, is *known* in laughter? A brief interlude might be valuable before considering this question, so that we can consider where we have come in the journey to understand humor. The emptiness of our original question, "What is humor?" has now been transformed into a more pointed question: "What is *known* in humor?" This is no small matter. We have arrived at a place where a pointed question can be addressed, with the hope that a more significant answer can be found.

Of course, our new question may not bear a great deal of fruit, either. One cursory examination would lead to the recognition that "what is known" in various forms of humor may vary. The laughing at slapstick or physical humor could be characterized as knowing "life is silly," or "taking yourself too seriously makes you a fool." In wisdom humor, there are deeper insights available. The knowing smile of the Buddha is not an indication that he knows that "life is silly"; it is not a goofy, childish smile, but that of a mature knowing that life is suffering, if we take the Buddhists seriously (pun recognized). Movement up the ladder of comedy may be quite similar to moving up the ladder of any other form of human endeavor. For example, a great deal of research has revealed the way in which moral development proceeds through a stage-like process. Why wouldn't humor follow a similar pattern of development?

There are many levels of humor—that much has certainly been apparent from this exploration. From the most primitive laughter associated with being tickled to the enjoyment of physical humor to the most sophisticated forms of irony or wisdom humor—we have seen that the nature of humor changes dramatically over many levels. Yet, strangely, we cannot but conclude that humor is still one thing. We know what is meant when we use the term. If one states, "That was not humorous," for example, we know what is being referred to. Humor, moreover, is one of the more advanced systems within human beings. It is just about the last to fully develop; in fact, we can say that most people never reach the level of appreciation for the highest forms of humor. The cleverness involved in sophisticated humor is most difficult to acquire. That is why it is so difficult to appreciate humor in a new language, even when the basics of that language have been mastered. Double meanings, incongruities, and ironies are quite esoteric—let alone the complexity involved in wisdom humor, especially for the novice.

Of course, the power of humor is increased as the level of humor increases. The effects of being tickled are temporary and fleeting, whereas the impact of a very powerful wisdom humor story can last a lifetime. The knowing smile of the guru represents something inherent in their very being, whereas the delight of the child who laughs at his friend's silly behavior has little endurance. Yet both provide transcendence. We can say, in fact, that the playful laughter of the chimpanzee provides a kind of transcendence, along with some powerful social functions. Because human beings require much more transcendence than other animals, though, we are not, ultimately, satisfied with humor that does not speak to the higher levels of our being.

We seek higher and higher levels of humor as we develop through the lifecycle. That is precisely why we condemn silliness in an adult as "childish" and find childish humor to be limited in its scope and less relevant to a fully developed adult. The development of forms of humor over the lifetime, however, is a project for another day or another scholar. What we have accomplished here, is having laid the groundwork for understanding the various forms of humor as well as constructing a kind of hierarchical typology that may be useful in understanding the differences between forms of humor.

Final Words

Humor is transcendence. It allows us to escape the seriousness of the moment and lift ourselves out of the situation we were embedded in and look at the world in a new light. This is why humor is a posture or position with respect to experience—a *comedic point of view*. Laughing is cheerful, optimistic, and freeing because it allows us to transcend the "within" and rise to a new place in which that limiting situation can be looked at and seen as limited. To not take a situation as seriously is to find a place beyond the demands and limitations of the situation as it presents itself. As that transcendence is elevated through higher levels of humor, moreover, it is the basis of a point of view that is embedded within wisdom. What began as the tickling of a small child develops into the ultimate form of a knowing smile.

REFERENCES

Abbott, B. & Costello, L. (2021). *Who's on first? Script* [TV transcript]. Abbott and Costello–Who's on First? https://abbott-and-costello-whos-on-first.info/whos-on-first-script/

Aharoni, R. (2018). Shifting from meaning to its carrier: A common denominator for three strains of humour. *European Journal of Humour Research, 6*(3), 13–29, https://doi.org/10.7592/EJHR2018.6.3.aharoni

Allan Sherman Channel. (2019, September 6). *Hello Muddah, Hello Fadduh (Camp Granada Song) with Lyrics Sing-Along, Allan Sherman, 1963, updated* [Video]. YouTube. https://www.youtube.com/watch?v=4yFTOvO0utY

Allen, W. (Director). (1973). *Sleeper.* [Film]. Jack Rollins & Charles H. Joffe Productions; Rollins-Joffe Productions.

Allen, W. (Director). (1977). *Annie Hall.* [Film]. Jack Rollins & Charles H. Joffe Productions; Rollins-Joffe Productions.

Allen, W. (1986). *Side effects.* Ballantine Books.

Ampoh. (2006, June 7). *Sam Kinison second appearance on Letterman* [Video]. YouTube. https://www.youtube.com/watch?v=qj9DdTXxDFU

AZ Quotes. (2021). *Daily Show Quotes.* https://www.azquotes.com/quotes/topics/daily-show.html

AZ Quotes. (2021). *Carol Leifer quotes.* AZ quotes. https://www.azquotes.com/author/21567-Carol_Leifer

AZ Quotes. (2021). *Wendy Liebman quotes.* https://www.azquotes.com/author/8858-Wendy_Liebman

AZ Quotes. (2021b). *Woody Allen.* https://www.azquotes.com/quote/549293

American Psychiatric Association. (2013). *Diagnostic and statistical manual of mental disorders* (5th ed.). https://doi.org/10.1176/appi.books.9780890425596

Andersen, H. C., Burton, V. L., & Houghton Mifflin Company. (1949). *The emperor's new clothes.* Houghton Mifflin Company.

Angeleri, R. & Airenti, G. (2014). The development of joke and irony understanding: A study with 3-to 6-year-old children. *Canadian Journal of Experimental Psychology*, 68(2), 133–146. https://doi.org/10.1037/cep0000011

Ardelt, M. (2003). Empirical assessment of a three-dimensional wisdom scale. *Research on Aging, 25*(3), 275–324. https://doi.org/10.1177/0164027503025003004

Aristotle. (1976). *The ethics of Aristotle: The Nicomachean ethics.* (A.K. Thomson, Trans.). Penguin Classics. (Original work published 340 BCE)

Atlas, G., Mastin, N., & Drake, C. (2015, August 6–9). *Individual differences in the experience, production, and function of humor in everyday life* [Poster presentation]. APA 2015 Convention, Toronto, Ontario, Canada.

Attardo, S., & Bell, N. (2010). Failed humor: Issues in non-native speakers' appreciation and understanding of humor. *Intercultural Pragmatics, 7*(3), 423–447. https://doi.org/10.1515/IPRG.2010.019

Ball, L. (2021). *Forbes quotes: thoughts on the business of life.* https://www.forbes.com/quotes/6176/

Baumeister, R. F., Schmeichel, B. J., & Vohs, K. D. (2007). Self-regulation and the executive function: The self as controlling agent. In A. W. Kruglanski & E. T. Higgins (Eds.), *Social psychology: Handbook of basic principles* (516–539). The Guilford Press.

Becker, E. (1973). *The denial of death.* Free Press.

Bippus, A. (2007). Factors predicting the perceived effectiveness of politicians' use of humor during a debate. *Humor: International Journal of Humor Research, 20*(2), 105–121. https://doi.org/10.1515/HUMOR.2007.006

Blakemore, S. J., Wolpert, D., & Frith, C. (2000). Why can't you tickle yourself? *Neuroreport, 11*(11), 11–16.

Bologna, C. (2017, May 18). *23 Times Tina Fey hilariously summed up parenting.* Huffpost. https://www.huffpost.com/entry/23-times-tina-fey-hilariously-summed-up-parenting_n_591a7d9de4b0809be15797ea

Brooks, M. (Director). (1974). *Blazing Saddles* [Film]. Crossbow Productions; Warner Bros.

Brooks, M. (Director). (1981). *History of the World: Part I* [Film]. Brooksfilms.

Brown, E. (2021). *Seeing and perceiving: A study of the use of disguised persons and wise fools in Shakespeare's plays.* Hassell Street Press.

Bruce, L. (2017, August 25). *Lenny Bruce: The Berkeley concert (1965)—transcript* [Transcript]. Scraps from the Loft. https://scrapsfromtheloft.com/comedy/lenny-bruce-berkeley-concert-1965-full-transcript/

Bruce, L. (1965/2016). *How to talk dirty and influence people.* Da Capo Press.

Bruckman, C. & Keaton, B. (Directors). (1926). *The General* [Film]. Buster Keaton Productions; Joseph M. Schenck Productions.

Caliendo, F. (2006, July 15). *Frank Caliendo Bush Impression.* [Video]. YouTube. https://www.youtube.com/watch?v=XK1ekhovFeU

Carroll, N. (2000). On Ted Cohen: Intimate laughter. *Philosophy and Literature, 24*(2), 435–450. Doi:10.1353/phl.2000.0029

Chaplin, C. (Director). (1931). *City lights* [Film]. Charles Chaplin Productions.

Chaplin, C. (Director). (1936). *Modern times* [Film]. Charles Chaplin Productions.

Chaplin, C. (Director). (1928). *The circus* [Film]. Charles Chaplin Productions.

Chaplin, C. (Director). (1925). *The gold rush* [Film]. Charles Chaplin Productions.

Chaplin, C. (Director). (1914). *The new janitor* [Film]. Keystone Film Company.

Cohen, T. (1999). *Jokes: Philosophical thoughts on joking matters.* University of Chicago Press.

Comicbook and Beyond. (2019, October 21). *130+ Punny jokes you can relate to.* https://comicbookandbeyond.com/punny-jokes

Cosby, B. (Director). (1983). *Bill Cosby: Himself.* [Film]. Bill Cosby; Jemmin Inc.

Cousins, N. (1979). *Anatomy of an illness as perceived by the patient: Reflections on healing and regeneration.* Open Road Integrated Media.

Creekmur, C. K. (2007). Brokeback: The parody. *GLQ: A Journal of Lesbian & Gay Studies, 13*(1), 105–107. https://muse.jhu.edu/article/207523/pdf

Dais, J. (2021, June 23). *The complete list of English idioms, proverbs, & expressions.* https://takelessons.com/blog/english-idioms

DannyTechWorld. (2012, July 2). *George Carlin – Euphemisms.* [Video]. YouTube. https://www.youtube.com/watch?v=isMm2vF4uFs

David, L., Garlin, J., Polone, G., Schaffer, J., Gibbons, T., O'Malley, E., Weide, R. B., Charles, L., Berg, A., & Mandel, D. (Executive Producers) (1999–2021). *Curb your enthusiasm* [TV series]. Home Box Office (HBO); Production Partners.

David, L., & Seinfeld, J. (Directors). (2013, June 13). I'm going to change your life forever (Season 2, Episode 1) [TV series]. In D. Tuohy & T. Johnston (Executive Producers), *Comedians in cars getting coffee.* Barry Katz Entertainment; Embassy Row; Sony Pictures Television.

David, L., & Seinfeld, J. (Directors). (2018, June 6). Tracy Morgan: Lasagna with six different cheeses (Season 10, Episode 4) [TV series]. In D. Tuohy & T. Johnston (Executive Producers), *Comedians in cars getting coffee.* Barry Katz Entertainment; Embassy Row; Sony Pictures Television.

De News (2016, April 30). The founder of Match.com, Gary Kremen, lost his girlfriend to a man she met on Match. *My Newspapers Online.* https://mynewspapersonline.blogspot.com/2016/04/the-founder-of-matchcom-gary-kremen.html

Deusner, S. M. (2009, November 16). *Never gets old: Carl Reiner & Mel Brooks, 'The 2,000 year old man: The complete history.'* The Washington Post. https://www.washingtonpost.com/express/wp/2009/11/16/carl-reiner-mel-brooks-2000-year-old-man/

Devereux, P. G., & Ginsburg, G. P. (2001). Sociality effects on the production of laughter. *Journal of General Psychology*, *128*(2), 227–240. https://doi.org/10.1080/00221300109598910

Dozois, D. J. A., Martin, R. A., & Faulkner, B. (2013). Early maladaptive schemas, styles of humor and aggression. *Humor: International Journal of Humor Research*, *26*(1), 97–116. https://doi.org/10.1515/humor-2013-0006

Duffy, M. E., & Teruggi, P. J. (2013). Does political humor matter? You betcha! Comedy TV's performance of the 2008 vice presidential debate. *Journal of Popular Culture*, *46*(3), 545-565. Doi:10.1111/jpcu.12038

Dyck, K. T. H., & Holtzman, S. (2013). Understanding humor styles and well-being: The importance of social relationships and gender. *Personality and Individual Differences*, *55*(1), 53–58. https://doi.org/10.1016/j.paid.2013.01.023

Ellis, A., & MacLaren, C. (1998). *Rational emotive behavior therapy: A therapist's guide.* Impact Publishers.

Erdodi, L & Lajiness-O'Neill, R. (2012). Humor perception in bilinguals: Is language more than a code? *Humor: International Journal of Humor Research*, *25*(4), 459–468. https://doi.org/10.1515/humor-2012-0024

Ferguson, M. A. & Ford, T. E. (2008). Disparagement humor: A theoretical and empirical review of psychoanalytic, superiority, and social identity theories. *Humor: International Journal of Humor Research*, *21*(3), 283–312. https://doi.org/10.1515/HUMOR.2008.014

Filani, I. (2017). "Laf wan kill me die" (I almost died laughing): An analysis of Akpos jokes and the readers' responses. *European Journal of Humour*, *4(4)*, 5–25. https://doi.org/10.7592/EJHR2016.4.4.filani

Forest, H. (1996). *Wisdom tales from around the world.* August House Publishers.

Freud, S. (1905/1960). Jokes and their relation to the unconscious. In J. Strachey (Ed. and Trans.), *The standard edition of the complete psychological works of Sigmund Freud* (8), (pp. 5–294). Hogarth Press.

Friedman, H. H. (2000). Humor in the Hebrew Bible. *Humor: International Journal of Humor Research*, *13*(3), 257–286. https://doi.org/10.1515/humr.2000.13.3.257

Gallagher. (2014, October 21). *Gallagher – Sledge-O-Matic (The Maddest)* [Video]. YouTube. https://www.youtube.com/watch?v=ErppAlOIGQE

Gallivan, J. (1999). Gender and humor: What makes a difference? *North American Journal of Psychology*, *1*(2), 307–318. https://www.proquest.com/openview/80dc8f-6931fa74618570d0fc4315b7f3/1.pdf?pq-origsite=gscholar&cbl=28796

Genius. (1996). *Ironic.* https://genius.com/Alanis-morissette-ironic-lyrics

Glamour. (2017, April 3). Amy Schumer's most controversial quotes. *Glamour.* https://www.glamourmagazine.co.uk/gallery/amy-schumer-best-controversial-quotes

Gollob, H. F. & Levine, J. (1967). Distraction as a factor in the enjoyment of aggressive humor. *Journal of Personality and Social Psychology, 5*(3), 368-372. https://doi.org/10.1037/h0024310

Goodreads. (2021). *Groucho Marx: Quotes: Quotable Quote.* https://www.goodreads.com/quotes/3730

Goodreads. (2021). *Rita Rudner: Quotes.* https://www.goodreads.com/author/quotes/79357.Rita_Rudner

Goodreads. (2021a). *Woody Allen.* https://www.goodreads.com/author/show/10356.Woody_Allen

Grunbaum, A. (1984). *The foundations of psychoanalysis: A philosophical critique.* University of California Press.

Gunner, J. (2021a). *Examples of verbal irony.* YourDictionary. https://examples.yourdictionary.com/examples-of-verbal-irony.html

Gunner, J. (2021b). *Dramatic irony examples in different media.* YourDictionary. https://examples.yourdictionary.com/dramatic-irony-examples.html

HahaHumor. (2021). *150 Very punny jokes that are the best form of humor ever.* https://www.hahahumor.com/very-funny-punny-jokes.

Hainsworth, P. & Robey, D. (2005). *The Oxford companion to Italian art.* Oxford University Press.

Hariman, R. (2007). In defense of Jon Stewart. *Critical Studies in Media Communication, 24*(3), 273–277. https://doi.org/10.1080/07393180701521031

Heidegger, M. (1962). *Being and time.* Harper & Row.

Hill, W. (Director). (1985). *Brewster's millions.* [Film]. Universal Pictures; Davis Entertainment; Lawrence Gordon Productions.

Holmes, D. S. (1969). Sensing humor: Latency and amplitude of response related to MMPI profiles. *Journal of Consulting and Clinical Psychology, 33*(3), 296–301. https://doi.org/10.1037/h0027581

Hu, R., Tosun, S., & Vaid, J. (2017). What's so funny? Modelling incongruity in humour production. *Cognition and Emotion, 31*(3), 484–499. https://doi.org/10.1080/02699931.2015.1129314

Husserl, E. (1900). *Logical investigations.* M. Niemeyer.

IGN. (2015). *The daily show with Jon Stewart.* https://www.ign.com/tv/the-daily-show

In5d. (2015, March 16). *97 Spiritual enlightenment stories.* https://in5d.com/97-spiritual-enlightenment-stories/

Irwin, W. (Ed.). (2000). *Seinfeld and philosophy: A book about everything and nothing.* Open Court Publishing.

Isen, A. M. (1987). Positive affect, cognitive processes, and social behavior. *Advances in Experimental Social Psychology, 20,* 203–253. https://doi.org/10.1016/S0065-2601(08)60415-3

Isha Institute. (2020, July 18). *Everything is empty—a Zen story.* https://isha.sadhguru.org/us/en/wisdom/article/everything-is-empty-zen-story

Ishijima, K., & Negayama, K. (2017). Development of mother-infant interaction in tickling play: The relationship between infants' ticklishness and social behaviors. *Infant Behavior & Development, 49,* 161–167. https://doi.org/10.1016/j.infbeh.2017.08.007

Johnson, E. (1949, November 2). Marx badgers contestants by John Crosby. *St. Petersburg Times,* 12.

Johnston, C. (1901). The essence of American humor. *The Atlantic Monthly, 87,* 195–202.

Jokes4us. (2021). *Marijuana jokes.* http://www.jokes4us.com/dirtyjokes/marijuanajokes.html

Jokes by Stephen Wright. (2021). *Part one: Wright knowledge.* http://www.wright-house.com/steven-wright/steven-wright-Kn.html

Kaartigan govindasamy. (2016, November 19). *Larry David interview 2016—Talk with Larry David.* [Video]. YouTube. https://www.youtube.com/watch?v=U6oW82OVQbU

Kafka, F. (1981). *The metamorphosis* (S. Corngold, Trans.). Bantam Books. (Original work published 1915)

Katiecotts22. (2007, December 13). *Bill Cosby Drinking.* [Video]. YouTube. https://www.youtube.com/watch?v=qYsko_tc3a0

Keillor, G. (2003). Introduction. In *A Prairie Home Companion: Pretty good joke book* (3rd ed., pp.7-9). High Bridge Company.

Keillor, G. (2005). Introduction. In *A Prairie Home Companion: Pretty good joke book.* (4th ed., pp.7-9). High Bridge Company.

Khan, N. I. (1939). *Twenty Jataka tales.* George G. Harrap and Co.

Khurana, S. (2019, July 30). 10 versions of Murphy's Law for universal 'truths.' *ThoughtCo.* https://www.thoughtco.com/murphys-laws-explain-unfathomable-truths-2832861

Kittelstad, K. (2021). *Examples of situational irony.* YourDictionary. https://examples.yourdictionary.com/examples-of-situational-irony.html

Kreuz, R. (2020). *Irony and sarcasm.* MIT Press.

Kronke, D. (1995, August 27). From the Archives: 'Oddball perfectionist' Garry Shandling on his constant quest to improve his craft. *Los Angeles Times.* https://www.latimes.com/entertainment/tv/showtracker/la-et-st-garry-shandling-profile-19950827-story.html

La Fave, L. (1972). Humor judgments as a function of reference groups and identification classes. In J. H. Goldstein & P. E. McGhee (eds.), *The psychology of humor: Theoretical perspectives and empirical issues* (pp. 195–210). Academic Press

La Fave, L., Haddad, J., & Marshall, N. (1974). Humor judgments as a function of identification classes. *Sociology and Social Research, 58*(1), 184–194.

La Fave, L., McCarthy, K. & Haddad, J. (1973). Humor judgments as a function of identification classes: Canadian vs. American. *Journal of Psychology, 85*(1), 53–59. https://doi.org/10.1080/00223980.1973.9923860

Lampert, M. D. & Ervin-Tripp, S. M. (1998). Exploring paradigms: The study of gender and sense of humor near the end of the 20th century. In W. Ruch (ed.), *The sense of humor: Explorations of a personality characteristic* (pp. 231–270). https://doi.org/10.1515/9783110804607.231

Lazarus, R. S. (1981). A cognitivist's reply to Zajonc on emotion and cognition. *American Psychologist,36*(2), 222–223. https://doi.org/10.1037/0003-066X.36.2.222

Lazarus, R. S. (1982). Thoughts on the relations between emotion and cognition. *American Psychologist, 37*(9), 1019–1024. https://doi.org/10.1037/0003-066X.37.9.1019

Lazarus, R. S. (1984). On the primacy of cognition. *American Psychologist, 39*(2), 124–129. https://doi.org/10.1037/0003-066x.39.2.124

Leavens, D. & Bard, K. (2006). Tickling. *Current Biology, 26*(3), 91–93. https://doi.org/10.1016/j.cub.2015.06.014.

Leibovich, M. (2008, October 5). Laugh, or the world laughs at you. *The New York Times.* https://www.nytimes.com/2008/10/05/world/ichael/05iht-05leibovich.16692711.html

Lewis, J. (Director). (1963). *The Nutty Professor* [Film]. Paramount Pictures; Jerry Lewis Films.

Lim, J. (Trans.). (1995). *100 Parables of Zen.* Asiapac Books.

Live from Here. (2019, March 19). *Jackie Kashian—Live from here.* [Video]. YouTube. https://www.youtube.com/watch?v=G-oV-js8RuM

Lubin, A. (Director). (1941). *Buck privates* [Film]. Universal Pictures.

Ludwig, D. (2014, July 9). Man who literally wrote the book on running with the bulls was gored by a bull. *The Atlantic.* https://www.theatlantic.com/international/archive/2014/07/man-who-wrote-the-book-on-running-with-the-bulls-is-gored-by-bull/374193/

Luebering, J. E. (n.d.) Slapstick. In *Britannica encyclopedia.* Retrieved February 20, 2022, from http://www.britannica.com/EBchecked/topic/548077/slapstick

Manku, G. (2008, August 7). *Everything comes to pass.* Gateways to Joy. https://gurmeet.net/inspiration/everything-comes-to-pass/

Markey, P. M., Suzuki, T. & Marino, D. P. (2014). The interpersonal meaning of humor styles. *Humor: International Journal of Humor Research, 27*(1), 47–64. https://doi.org/10.1515/humor-2013-0052

Marshall, A.W. & Marshall, G. (Executive Producers). (1978–1982). *Mork and Mindy* [TV series]. Henderson Productions; Miller-Milkis Productions; Paramount Television.

Martin, R. A. (2001). Humor, laughter, and physical health: Methodological issues and research findings. *Psychological Bulletin, 127*(4), 504–519. https://doi.org/10.1037/0033-2909.127.4.504

Martin, R. A. (2007). *The psychology of humor: An integrative approach.* Elsevier Academic Press.

Martin, R. A., and Ford, T. (2018). *The psychology of humor: An integrative approach* (2nd ed.). Elsevier Academic Press.

Martin, S. (2008). *Born standing up: A comic's life*. Scribner.

McCollum, H. & White, J. (Producers). (1930–1970). *The three stooges* [TV series]. Fox Film Corporation, Mentone Productions, Columbia Pictures Corporation, Normandy Film Corporation, & Cambria Studios Productions.

McGhee, P. E. & Duffey, N. S. (1983). The role of identity of the victim in the development of disparagement humor. *Journal of General Psychology, 108*(2), 257–275. https://doi.org/10.1080/00221309.1983.9711499

McRae, J. (2003). Beginnings: Differentiating/Connecting Bodhidharma and the East Mountain Teaching. In *Seeing through Zen: Encounter, transformation, and genealogy in Chinese Chan Buddhism* (pp. 22). University of California Press.

Merleau-Ponty, M. (1962). *Phenomenology of perception*. Routledge.

Merriam-Webster (n.d.). Irony. In *Merriam-Webster.com dictionary*. Retrieved February 20, 2022. https://www.merriam-webster.com/dictionary/irony

Merriam-Webster (n.d.). Parody. In *Merriam-Webster.com dictionary*. Retrieved February 20, 2022. https://www.merriam-webster.com/dictionary/parody

Merriam-Webster (n.d.). Sarcasm. In *Merriam-Webster.com dictionary*. Retrieved February 20, 2022. https://www.merriam-webster.com/dictionary/sarcasm

Merriam-Webster (n.d.). Satire. In *Merriam-Webster.com dictionary*. Retrieved February 20, 2022. https://www.merriam-webster.com/dictionary/satire

Mickes, L., Walker, D. E., Parris, J. L., Mankoff, R., & Christenfeld, N. (2012). Who's funny: Gender stereotypes, humor production, and memory bias. *Psychonomic Bulletin & Review, 19*(1), 108–112. https://psycnet.apa.org/doi/10.3758/s13423-011-0161-2

Middleton, R. (1959). Negro and white reactions to racial humor. *Sociometry, 22*(2), 175–183. https://doi.org/10.2307/2786021

Milgram, S. (1963). Behavioral study of obedience. *Journal of Abnormal and Social Psychology, 67*(4), 371–378. https://doi.org/10.1037/h0040525

Miller, S.L., Maner, J.K., & Becker, D.V. (2010). Self-protective biases in group categorization: Threat cues shape the psychological boundary between "us" and "them." *Journal of Personality and Social Psychology, 99*(1), 62–77. https://doi.org/10.1037/a0018086

Morreall, J. (1983). *Taking laughter seriously*. State University of New York Press.

Morreall, J. (1987). *The philosophy of laughter and humor*. State University of New York Press.

Morreall, J. (2001). Sarcasm, irony, wordplay, and humor in the Hebrew Bible: A response to Hershey Friedman. *Humor: International Journal of Humor Research*, 14(3), 293–301. https://doi.org/10.1515/humr.2001.005

Morreall, J. (2009). *Comic relief: A comprehensive philosophy of humor*. Wiley.

Murphy's Laws Site. (2021). *All the laws of Murphy in one place.* http://www.murphys-laws.com/murphy/murphy-laws.html

Namaste Publishing. (2016, March 9). *Eckhart Tolle laughter breaks through the ego* [Video]. YouTube. https://www.youtube.com/watch?v=nyUG5KnutTo

Nevo, O., Nevo, B., & Leong, J. S. Y. (2001). Singaporean humor: A cross-cultural, cross-gender comparison. *The Journal of General Psychology, 128*(2), 143–156. https://doi.org/10.1080/00221300109598904

Phillips, M. (2010, Oct. 14). 'Jackass' slapstick no special effect. *Chicago Tribune.* https://www.chicagotribune.com/entertainment/ct-xpm-2010-10-14-sc-mov-1015-jackass-3d-20101015-story.html

Plato. (369 B.C./1990). Jowett, B. (Trans.). *Theaetetus.* New York: C. Scribner's Sons

Plato. (375 B.C./1943). *Plato's The Republic.* New York: Books, Inc.

Post Randomonium. (2021). *Funny status.* https://www.postrandomonium.com/Status/16004

Provine, R. R. (2004). Laughing, tickling, and the evolution of speech and self. *Current Directions In Psychological Science, 13*(6), 215–218. https://doi.org/10.1111/j.0963-7214.2004.00311.x

Punpedia. (2021). Funny puns. https://punpedia.org/funny-puns/

Rapp, A. (1951). *The origins of wit and humor.* Dutton.

Reddit (n.d.). *Oneliners* [Reddit forum]. Retrieved on February 20, 2022. https://www.reddit.com/r/oneliners

Reddit (n.d.). *Jokes: Get your funny on!* [Reddit forum]. Retrieved February 20, 2022. https://www.reddit.com/r/Jokes

Regan, B. (2012). *All by myself.* ASIN: B00PUTM6VC

Regan, B. (2018, January 28). *Brian Regan: Nunchucks and flamethrowers (2017)—full transcript* [Transcript]. Scraps from the Loft. https://scrapsfromtheloft.com/comedy/brian-regan-nunchucks-flamethrowers-transcript/

Reiner, C. (Writer), Rick, J. (Director). (1962, January 3). Where did I come from? (Season 1, Episode 15) [TV series episode]. In L. Sheldon & D. Thomas (Executive Producers), *The Dick Van Dyke show.* Calvada Productions.

Reiser, P. (1994). *Couplehood.* Bantam Books.

Rogoff, R. (2014, July 4). He drives at night. *Pleasanton Weekly.* https://pleasantonweekly.com/blogs/p/2014/07/04/he-drives-at-night

Rorty, R. (1982). *Consequences of pragmatism.* University of Minnesota Press.

Ruch, W. (1998). *The sense of humor: Explorations of a personality characteristic.* Mouton de Gruyter.

Ryan, Jr., F. J. (2004, May 25). *Ronald Reagan Presidential Oral History Project*. Miller Center of Public Affairs. Retrieved February 20, 2022, http://web1.millercenter.org/poh/transcripts/ohp_2004_0525_ryan.pdf

Sager, J. (2021, February 10). *125 George Carlin quotes to make you laugh, smile, and think*. Parade. https://parade.com/1080754/jessicasager/george-carlin-quotes/

Sartre, J. (1943). *Being and nothingness: An essay on phenomenological ontology*. Taylor & Francis.

Savage, B.M., Lujan, H.L., Thipparthi, R.R., & DiCarlo, S.E. (2017). Humor, laughter, learning, and health! A brief review. *Advances in Physiology Education, 41*(3), 341–347. https://doi.org/10.1152/advan.00030.2017

Scarlet Fever. (2005, September 2). *Michael Moore open letter to Bush*. https://www.scarletfever.org/forum/ichael-moore-open-letter-to-bush_topic4659.html

Schaier, A.H. & Cicirelli, V.G. (1976). Age differences in humor comprehension and appreciation in old age. *Journal of Gerontology, 31*(5), 577–582. https://doi.org/10.1093/geronj/31.5.577

Scott M. (2018, October 24). Wanda Sykes' jokes about relationships that will make you laugh out loud. *Amomama*. https://news.amomama.com/113953-wanda-sykes-jokes-relationships.html

Sedgwick, E. (Director). (1932). *Passionate plumber* [Film]. Metro-Goldwyn-Mayer (MGM).

Seed, A. (2015). *The funny book of weird and wacky words*. Bloomsbury Publishing.

Searles, C. (1925). The first six decades of French 17th century comedy. *Modern Philology, 23*(2), 153–165. http://www.jstor.org/stable/433678

Sedgwick, E. (Director). (1930). *Free and easy* [Film]. Metro-Goldwyn-Mayer (MGM).

Sedgwick, E. (Director). (1931). *Parlor, bedroom, and bath* [Film]. Metro-Goldwyn-Mayer (MGM).

Shadyac, T. (Director). (1996). *The nutty professor* [Film]. Imagine Entertainment.

Shah, I. (1978, April). *The wisdom of Sufic humor (from Human Nature, April 1978)*. http://www.katinkahesselink.net/sufi/sufi-jok.html

Shammi, P. & Stuss, D. T. (2003). The effects of normal aging on humor appreciation. *Journal of the International Neuropsychological Society, 9*(6), 855–863. doi:10.1017/S135561770396005X

Stephens, P. (2014, June 27). Gelotophobia: Living a life in fear of laughter. *BBC News*. https://www.bbc.com/news/health-27323470

Suresha, R.J. (2014). *Extraordinary adventures of Mullah Nasruddin: Naughty, unexpurgated stories of the beloved wise fool from the Middle and Far East*. Lethe Press.

Swani, K., Weinberger, M. G., & Gulas, C. S. (2013). The impact of violent humor on advertising success: A gender perspective. *Journal of Advertising, 42*(4), 308–319. https://doi.org/10.1080/00913367.2013.795121

Swatzwelder, J. (2004). *The time machine did it.* Kennydale Books.

Swift, J. (2020). *A modest proposal.* East India Publishing Company. (Original work published 1729)

Taylor, M., Bates, G., & Webster, J. D. (2011). Comparing the psychometric properties of two measures of wisdom: Predicting forgiveness and psychological well-being with the Self-Assessed Wisdom Scale (SAWS) and the Three-Dimensional Wisdom Scale (3D-WS). *Experimental Aging Research, 37*(2), 129–141. https://doi.org/10.1080/0361 073X.2011.554508

The Best Quotations. (2022). *Quotes by Phyllis Diller.* https://best-quotations.com/authquotes.php?auth=1884

The Late Show with Stephen Colbert. (2016, May 25). *Lewis Black yells at your roommate.* [Video]. YouTube. https://www.youtube.com/watch?v=M4xQeFMtG4E

Tremaine, J. (Director). (2006). *Jackass number two* [Film]. Paramount Pictures, MTV Films, Dickhouse Productions, & Lynch Siderow Productions.

Tremaine, J. (Director). (2010). *Jackass 3D* [Film]. Dickhouse Productions, Film Roman Productions, & MTV Films.

The Epistle. (2021). God will save me. *The Epistle.* http://epistle.us/inspiration/godwillsaveme.html

Tremaine, J. (Director). (2002). *Jackass: The movie* [Film]. Paramount Pictures, MTV Films, Dickhouse Productions, Lynch Siderow Productions, and Viacom International.

Tremaine, J. (Director). (2006). *Jackass number two* [Film]. Paramount Pictures, MTV Films, Dickhouse Productions, & Lynch Siderow Productions.

Tremaine, J. (Director). (2010). *Jackass 3D* [Film]. Dickhouse Productions, Film Roman Productions, & MTV Films.

Upjoke. (n.d.). *Inmate jokes.* Retrieved February 20, 2022, from https://upjoke.com/inmate-jokes

Upjoke. (n.d.). *Nudist jokes.* Retrieved February 20, 2022, from https://upjoke.com/nudist-jokes

Urbisci, R. (Director). (2001). *George Carlin: Complaints and grievances* [Film]. Cable Stuff Productions.

Voltaire. (1975). *Candide.* Random House. (Original work published 1759)

Watson, K. (2011). Gallows humor in medicine. *The Hastings Center Report, 41*(5), 37–45. doi: 10.1002/j.1552-146x.2011.tb00139.x

Webster, J. D. (2007). Measuring the character strength of wisdom. *International Journal of Aging and Human Development, 65*(2), 163–183. https://doi.org/10.2190/AG.65.2.d

Weisfeld, G. E. (2006). Humor appreciation as an adaptive esthetic emotion. *Humor: International Journal of Humor Research, 19*(1), 1–26. https://doi.org/10.1515/HUMOR.2006.001

Westbury, C., & Hollis, G. (2019). Wriggly, squiffy, lummox, and boobs: What makes some words funny? *Journal of Experimental Psychology: General, 148*(1), 97–123. https://doi.org/10.1037/xge0000467

Whitehead, A. N. (2001). *Dialogues of Alfred North Whitehead, as recorded by Lucien Price.* Little, Brown Publishers. (Original work published 1954)

Whitehead, A. & Russell, B. (1925). *Principia Mathematica.* Cambridge University Press.

Wicker, F.W., Thorelli, I.M., Barron, W.L., & Willis, A.C. (1981). Studies of mood and humor appreciation. *Motivation and Emotion, 5*(1), 47–59. https://doi.org/10.1007/BF00993661

Winkie, L. (2020). *21 of the funniest and most unforgettable Mitch Hedberg jokes.* Vulture. https://www.vulture.com/2020/02/best-mitch-hedberg-jokes.html

Wright, S. (1985). *I have a pony* [Album]. Warner Bros. Records.

Weinbender, N. (2016, January 7). Wright trolls life for humor. *The Spokesman Review.* https://www.spokesman.com/stories/2016/jan/07/choice-words-wright-trolls-life-for-humor/

Wyer, R. S., & Collins, J. E. (1992). A theory of humor elicitation. *Psychological Review, 99*(4), 663–688. https://doi.org/10.1037/0033-295x.99.4.663

Yoon, H.J. (2018). Creating the mood for humor: Arousal level priming in humor advertising. *The Journal of Consumer Marketing, 35*(5), 491–501. https://doi.org/10.1108/JCM-01-2017-2074

Zajonc, R. B. (1980). Feeling and thinking: Preferences need no inferences. *American Psychologist, 35*(2), 151–175. https://doi.org/10.1037/0003-066X.35.2.151

Zajonc, R. B. (1981). A one-factor mind about mind and emotion. *American Psychologist, 36*(1), 102–103. https://doi.org/10.1037/0003-066X.36.1.102

Zajonc, R. B. (1984). On the primacy of affect. *American Psychologist, 39*(2), 117–123. https://doi.org/10.1037/0003-066X.39.2.117

Zhan, L. (2012). Understanding humor based on the incongruity theory and the cooperative principle. *Studies in Literature and Language, 4*(2), 94–98. https://doi.org/10.3968/j.sll.1923156320120402.3521

Zinkhan, G. M. & Gelb, B. D. (1990). Repetition, social settings, perceived humor, and wearout. *Advances in Consumer Research, 17*(1), 438–441. https://www.acrwebsite.org/volumes/7045/volumes/v17/NA-17

Ziv, A. (2010). The social function of humor in interpersonal relationships. *Society, 47,* 11–18. https://doi.org/10.1007/s12115-009-9283-9

ABOUT THE AUTHOR

Dr. Gordon Atlas is professor emeritus at Alfred University in New York. He received his BA in philosophy from S.U.N.Y. Binghamton and his MSW and PhD in Personality Psychology from the University of Michigan. He taught in the Psychology Division at Alfred University for thirty years.

Dr. Atlas was the recipient of five "Excellence in Teaching" awards from Alfred University. He served as the Director of the Honors Program at Alfred for ten years. He has published numerous articles in professional journals and has delivered several lectures as an invited speaker at other universities.

Most relevant to this book, Dr. Atlas taught a seminar on the Psychology of Comedy on a consistent basis at Alfred University.

He has always been fascinated by humor, and while teaching the Comedy course, he constructed the basic format and content of the book through that experience. Dr. Atlas also conducted his own research on the "hilariously funny," studying participants' personal examples of the absolutely funniest experiences of their lives.

Dr. Atlas resides in Key West, Florida, with his wife, Jana. There he is able to enjoy several of his passions—snorkeling and underwater photography, live music, and writing.

The author can be contacted by email at: gda94@yahoo.com.

www.ingramcontent.com/pod-product-compliance
Lightning Source LLC
Chambersburg PA
CBHW061730120626
46550CB00005B/1758